WOMAN TO WOMAN

An Anthology of Women's Spiritualities

Phyllis Zagano

A Michael Glazier Book
THE LITURGICAL PRESS
Collegeville, Minnesota

A Michael Glazier Book published by The Liturgical Press

Cover design by David Manahan, O.S.B.
Cover art: Scala/Art Resource, NY
 1. S0007863 K 70853   Color Transp.
 Albertinelli, Mariotto: Visitation (detail). Florence, Uffizi.

3	4	5	6	7	8	9

Library of Congress Cataloging-in-Publication Data

Woman to woman : an anthology of women's spiritualities / Phyllis
  Zagano.
      p.   cm.
   "A Michael Glazier book."
   Includes bibliographical references.
   ISBN 0-8146-5025-2
   1. Women, Catholic—Religious life.   2. Spiritual life—Catholic
authors.   I. Zagano, Phyllis.
BX2347.8.W6W66   1993
248'.082—dc20
                                              93-18865
                                                CIP

To my friends
Irene and Marjorie,
true companions on the journey

Contents

Acknowledgments

THE CROSSROAD PUBLISHING COMPANY
Texts from *Beguine Spirituality: Mystical Writings of Mechthild of Magdeburg, Beatrice of Nazareth and Hadewijch of Brabant,* edited and introduced by Fiona Bowie. Introduction compilation copyright © Fiona Bowie 1989. Translation copyright © Oliver Davies 1989. Reprinted by permission of The Crossroad Publishing Company.

HARPERCOLLINS PUBLISHERS, INC.
Excerpts from *Loaves and Fishes* by Dorothy Day. Copyright © 1963 by Harper & Row, Publishers, Inc. Reprinted by permission of HarperCollins Publishers.

ICS PUBLICATIONS
Texts from *The Collected Works of Edith Stein, Volume Two, Essays on Woman* translated by Freda Mary Oben, Ph.D. © 1987 Washington Province of Discalced Carmelites, Inc. ICS Publications, 2121 Lincoln Road, N.E., Washington, DC 20002 U.S.A. Reprinted by permission of ICS Publications.

INSTITUTUM BEATAE MARIAE VIRGINIS
Texts from the writings of Mary Ward from the Institute Archives in Munich. Used by permission of the Institute Beatae Mariae Virginis, Rome, Italy. Translation copyright © 1992 by Phyllis Zagano.

MARQUETTE UNIVERSITY ARCHIVES
Texts from the unpublished letters of Jessica Powers to Margaret Ellen Traxler, S.S.N.D. Used by permission of the Carmel of the Mother of God, Pewaukee, Wisconsin, and Sr. Margaret Ellen Traxler, S.S.N.D.

MARYKNOLL MISSION ARCHIVES
Texts from the unpublished letters of Ita Ford, M.M. Used by permission of the Maryknoll Sisters of St. Dominic, Inc., Maryknoll, N.Y.

PAULIST PRESS
Texts from *Hildegard of Bingen-Scivias,* trans. Mother Columba Hart and Jane Bishop (Mahwah, N.J.: Paulist Press, 1990). Copyright © 1990 by the Abbey of Regina Laudis: Benedictine Congregation Regina Laudis of the Strict Observance, Inc. Reprinted by permission of Paulist Press.

Texts from *Julian of Norwich: Showings,* trans. and intro. Edmund Colledge, O.S.A. and James Walsh, S.J. (Mahwah, N.J.: Paulist Press, 1978). Copyright 1978 by The Missionary Society of St. Paul the Apostle in the State of New York. Reprinted by permission of Paulist Press.

Texts from *Catherine of Siena-The Dialogue,* trans. Suzanne Noffke, O.P. (Mahwah, N.J.: Paulist Press, 1980). Copyright © 1980 by The Missionary Society of St. Paul the Apostle in the State of New York. Reprinted by permission of Paulist Press.

Texts from *Teresa of Avila: The Interior Castle*, Kieran Kavanaugh and Otilio Rodriguez, trans. © 1979 by the Washington Province of Discalced Carmelites, Inc. Used by permission of Paulist Press.

THE PUTNAM PUBLISHING GROUP
Texts from *Waiting for God* by Simone Weil. Copyright © 1951 by Simone Weil. Reprinted by permission of The Putnam Publishing Group.

SHEED & WARD
Poems from *Selected Poetry of Jessica Powers*, edited by Regina Siegfried and Robert Morneau. Copyright © 1989 by Sheed & Ward. Used by permission of Sheed & Ward, Inc.

SISTERS OF CHARITY OF ST. VINCENT DE PAUL OF NEW YORK
Texts from the unpublished letters of Mother Elizabeth Ann Bayley Seton. Used by permission of the Archives of the Sisters of Charity of St. Vincent de Paul of New York.

THE SOCIETY FOR THE PROMOTION OF CHRISTIAN KNOWLEDGE
Texts from *Julian of Norwich: Showings*, trans. and intro. Edmund Walsh, O.S.A., and James Walsh, S.J. (London: SPCK, 1978). Reprinted by permission of SPCK.

PHYLLIS ZAGANO
Translation of letter 52 from *Lettres Chretiennes et Spirituelles sur divers Sujets qui regardent La Vie Interieure ou L'ésprit du vrai Christianisme*, London, 1768. Translation copyright © 1992 by Phyllis Zagano.

Preface

It is impossible to recall how the conversations of a lifetime coalesce into a single book or project. My own lifelong interest in the spiritual advice women give other women is formed and fed by the advice I have received along the way, either in person or in writing, from women I know and from women I will never meet. Most of that advice has been superb, graced with reverence and with joy. Some of it has missed the mark. The reader is surely aware that in asking for assistance, it helps not to be a moving target.

The proximate preparation for this book began in earnest in November 1991, shortly after my conversations with Mary Milligan, R.S.H.M., professor of theology at Loyola-Marymount University, Los Angeles, at the Annual Meeting of the American Academy of Religion in Kansas City. She sparked hope in a cold Kansas night and generously followed the projects from start to finish. She joins the new friends and old I thank for their contributions to the research and writing. Those whom I have overlooked, or whose generous acts of friendship are privileged, join in fact if not in name those listed here below.

For sharing his enduring and endearing knowledge of Rome, and for recalling with me details about Catherine of Siena, I am grateful to John E. Fanning of the metropolitan tribunal of the archdiocese of New York.

For their gracious reception in Rome, and for helping me with the selections from the writings of their foundress, Mary Ward, I am indebted to Immolata Wetter, I.B.M.V., and Bernadette Ganne, I.B.M.V., archivists of the Institutum Beatae Mariae Virginis in Rome.

For standing by me in so many of my battles, most recently with the French of Mme. Jeanne Marie Guyon, I am indebted to Peter J. Houle of New York City.

For assistance with the papers of Elizabeth Seton, I thank Rita King, S.C., archivist, and Anne Courtney, S.C., former archivist of the Sisters of Charity, New York City. For her knowledge of her foundress and for her constant charity, I thank both God and Mary Sweeney, S.C., assistant chaplain of Newman House, Boston University, Boston.

For advice and instruction on Dorothy Day, I thank Nancy L. Roberts, associate professor of journalism at the University of Minnesota.

For sharing Jessica Powers' letters and for her support of this project, I am indebted to Margaret Ellen Traxler, S.S.N.D., CEO of the Institute of Women Today, Chicago. For their professional assistance and trust, I am grateful to Charles Elston, archivist, and Phil Runkle, assistant archivist, Marquette University Libraries, Milwaukee.

For helping me understand the life of my near contemporary, Ita Ford, I thank Elizabeth Yakel, director, Maryknoll Mission Archives, Maryknoll, N.Y., as I applaud her professionalism.

For providing me with libraries that work, I am constantly indebted to Boston University and to John Laucus, librarian of Boston University. To him and to that university's librarians and inter-library loan officers, without whom this project would have failed, I repeat my many thanks.

For their cheerful assistance during the spring '92 semester, I thank Lynn Taylor and Alfred Drears, my graduate assistants at the Boston University College of Communication.

And because they constantly encourage me to keep dreaming, I have dedicated this work of academic year '91–'92 to Irene Kelly, R.S.H.M., and Marjorie Keenan, R.S.H.M., true companions on the journey.

There is much to be said about spiritual friendship in the pages that follow. The women who wrote the words I have collected had at the core of their being a sense of the dignity of the other, the beauty of the person, and a reverence for the delicacy of relationships that makes each one of them an individual we would like to know better. Each presents for us an example of the kind of counselor at whose feet we might sit, if only for a little while, secure in the knowledge that she would gently meet the work of the Lord within us with patience, with gratitude, and with respect.

August 27, 1992
Feast of St. Monica
New York City

Introduction

The perplexities of life, in any era, often cloud the intuitive and contemplative faculties of women. For whatever reason, we are inevitably drawn to the complexities of the day— arts, politics, finance—through our husbands, our communities, our careers, or our causes. We are swept into the web of belief that action is always preferable to inaction, that doing is always preferable to being. We are compelled to do something, anything, in support of what we hold to be true, yet we are torn between the Mary and the Martha of the Gospel. The paradox, of course, is that "being," whether understood as being holy or as being in love, cannot exist without some sort of "doing," usually action outside the self in the service of another.

This is the connection between prayer and service. Often the doing that comes of inaction—the contemplative turning over of the self and all others to the care of God—is more "active" than any external activity performed in the same service. Without prayerful inaction, we can never be sure when action is best; without prayerful being, we can never be sure when doing is called for. So we face the unending need to reevaluate our inner lives and our spiritualities, our relations with God, and our relations with the world.

It is often a startling rediscovery to learn that we can reevaluate our spiritualities without losing who we are. In fact, it is in the reevaluation that we rediscover and reaffirm our very selves. This book is born of my own reevaluations and my own conscious effort to hear what women have been saying over the years, to me and to each one of us, about the ways of being and of doing that form our day-to-day existence.

The women whose writing makes up the bulk of this book are different colors in the wonderful kaleidoscope of history. Their works are arranged chronologically, beginning with Hildegard of Bingen in the eleventh century and moving to Ita Ford in our own. They are not all mystics; they are not all contemplatives; they are not all abbesses, or founders, or mothers, or secular champions of the faith. They are all different while they are all the same. They are icons of women through the centuries who have loved and loved deeply their husbands, their communities, their careers or their causes, but who, most of all, loved God.

That love expressed is one of the themes that forms the backdrop for the selections. Service of the Church, often understood in terms of a female diaconate, is the action born of contemplation. Many contend an actual diaconate of women was present in the early centuries of the western Church and known in the eastern Church until approximately the eleventh century when these selections begin. By then, with few exceptions, all the possible or potential ways of consecration and service for women were conflated into enclosed life in monasteries. The orders of deacons, widows, virgins and others died out; enclosure was the primary choice.

One enclosed woman, Hildegard of Bingen (1098–1179) wrote widely and well on multiple topics, but she opens this work with a small paragraph on choice. Centuries before Ignatian "discernment" became the order of the day for religious women, Hildegard explained the manner of choice and election. The choice can only be affirmed by love, and that love is the love of God as described by Beatrice of Nazareth (1200–1268). Whatever that choice, it is supported by the complementarity and polarity of faith and zeal, the one supporting and developing the other in the service of God, as Gertrude the Great (1256–1302) tells us.

The acceptance of the call to live in faith and zeal often

leads to consecration in a particular way. Enclosure in monastic communities neither was nor is attractive to all called to life with God; it neither was nor is conducive to every individual prayer life. The English anchorite Julian of Norwich (1342–1423) lived alone as mystic in her anchorhold, celebrating the God who touched her, and here reminds us that the only and ultimate trust one must retain is trust in God. All that is exists within the hand of God, we have only to recognize this to be able to accept God's care for us. Catherine of Siena (1347–1380) is also a solitary and a mystic, but she blends two vocations: active and contemplative life. Her choice finds her gently accepting of those whom she serves, her exterior living of the Word of God the result of her having humbly received it.

The complementarity of active and contemplative life presents itself interiorly as well, in the life of prayer. Teresa of Avila (1515–1582), Carmelite reformer and foundress, speaks to the original question: the relationship of the woman with God. Perseverance in prayer, a recommendation of each of these women, is a particular recommendation of hers. Later, Jane Frances de Chantal (1572–1641), who set out to found an active community but bowed to ecclesiastical pressure for enclosure, recommends simplicity in all relations, most particularly with God in prayer. Utmost trust is needed for such simplicity, and Mary Ward (1585–1645), who spent two-thirds of her life seeking a way for women contemplatives to act in the world, warns of the long loneliness in such an endeavor as she explains her constant trust in the Lord.

The inextricable bond of being and doing moves from Mary Ward to Jeanne Marie Guyon (1648–1717), who teaches abandonment in prayer as the methodology for action, and to Elizabeth Seton (1774–1821), who centers such abandoned prayer, and belief, in the ultimate passive act, the mystery of Eucharist.

The modern era sends forth the Mary/Martha of us all, either in prayerful or in actual involvement with the world's trials. Edith Stein (1891–1942) is the public scholar who becomes a cloistered nun, yet she tells us there is nothing that a woman cannot do. Her contemporary, Dorothy Day (1897–1980), seems to prove this point, and she is stern in her understanding of poverty as that which frees the soul for the combination of inaction and action in a life of prayer and service, no matter how it is led. Jessica Powers (1905–1988), poet and prioress, is simple and self-effacing, wholly given to the Lord and teaching an understanding of chastity that every woman can recognize and savor; it is only through the gift of self that one's self becomes ratified, disappearing in the Wholly Other while remaining intact. There appears to be a withholding of self in Simone Weil (1909–1943), but we can consider the possibility that in obedience to the self she had given away, she could not have what seemed to call her so deeply through the Eucharist: an inculturated faith that she did not inherit. She calls us to examine obedience, which is real and which leads to holiness when it addresses the deepest issues of self. Arguably, the ultimate holiness is simply dealing with reality, something Ita Ford (1940–1980) did in her writing and in her life. She speaks here about vocation, every woman's vocation, which is to find and to cherish and to live and to love that which resonates within her heart.

In some ways the women here flow from a great river of women, enclosed until the fourteenth century, breaking out in later centuries either to be enclosed alone or to prayerfully walk the highways in service, then moving to be enclosed with God either alone in the world, or in a contemplative community, or in an active community. They show the various facets of the cut crystal of our individual lives, each able to reflect with deeper beauty the wonderful, gratuitous gift of life and love we each receive by simply opening our hearts and minds and looking toward the Lord.

This volume spans a thousand years or so of the history of spirituality, presenting women mystics, contemplatives, actives, intellectuals, poets, and dreamers. It is a text which shows the major movements within women's hearts through the centuries. Since the primary anthologies in spirituality are anthologies of mysticism, it finds a broader base both historically and systematically. This book might do well as a companion to other selections in a history of spirituality course or to any of a number of courses where the experience of women is the focus.

It is also a commonplace book filled with favorite passages, and from start to finish it can bring the reader through the stages of vocational decision-making we all go through at various times, or at least each time, like Abraham, we must pick up and simply go. There is no external answer at the end, no ready-made solution for the personal puzzle, for the book closes in this century with a Jewish-born Carmelite nun and scholar, an Anglican-born deeply Catholic secular woman, a mid-western Carmelite nun and poet, a brilliant philosopher who professes no formal faith, and a Catholic apostolic religious. They are as individual as the reader, who no doubt will find herself in each of them.

Perhaps the primary criterion for each selection that follows was whether I could read it, out loud, to someone who came to me for advice or assistance on its topic. Each passage has been consciously chosen to accompany an individual in affirming and reaffirming her choices, perhaps providing the sort of experience and common sense, and respect for the uniqueness of the individual, that is often so difficult to find.

Overall the book stands as an argument to choose whatever is life-giving and filled with hope, to freely seek advice, and to freely discard it if it cannot be absorbed alone before the Lord. It is important to keep searching—to look, to ask, to pray—and to recognize all along that the most important thing is to choose life: to choose prayerfully, actively, joyfully and honestly, and never, ever, to give up the dream.

Hildegard of Bingen (1098–1179)

Hildegard of Bingen, a sickly child who grew to be a mystic, a visionary, and a prophet, was placed by her family in the care of Jutta, a recluse at Disibodenberg, near Speyer, in Germany when she was eight years old. A community formed there, and as a teenager Hildegard chose to live in vows according to the Rule of St. Benedict. When Jutta died in 1136, Hildegard became abbess of the monastery. She eventually founded two others, one in 1147, another in 1165.

She was writer, exegete, composer and preacher, and correspondent of all the major Church leaders of her day, from Bernard of Clairvaux to Thomas Becket, through four popes (Eugene III, Anastasius IV, Adrian IV, and Alexander III), as well as with royalty from Greece, England, and Germany. She wrote mystical treatises, books of medicine and medicinal remedies, liturgical poetry, music and ethics, as well as homilies, a morality play, and *Lingua ignota*, a book about a secret language.

At forty-two Hildegard received a vision in a brilliant light, illuminating the mysteries of the Gospels and the psalter for her heart and her mind. From that time on, for the next ten years, she wrote down twenty-six of her visions and her understandings of the love between God and humanity in creation, redemption, and the Church in her famous *Scivias*. Her spiritual writings were approved as authentic by Archbishop Henry of Mainz and again by Bishop Albero of Chiny (on the order of Pope Eugene III), and she drew crowds from all over France and Germany who came for her guidance.

She was derided as the "Sibyl of the Rhine" but recognized as a sage and a prophet. While she has been venerated, she has never been officially declared a saint (which process was reserved to the Holy See by her contemporary Alexander III in 1171). This is quite probably the result of her row with Church authority during the last year of her life, when she allowed an excommunicated young man to be buried in a cemetery adjoining her abbey. Her defense, that he had received the last rites, was not accepted, and the convent was put under the censure of interdict.

The wonderful truth she teaches in the following selection is that it is in the mind that we know God and choose his will for us. When we choose aright, we are well aware of it, in fact we "feel" it. The choice thus confirmed in fact confirms itself, for it is of an act "productive and perfect and prosperous; and the fiery grace of Christ Jesus calls this to the person's mind anew."

Scivias, Number 32

The first root of human choice and the fiery grace of Christ

Now, therefore, O human, understand and learn. From whence do these things come? What does this mean? It is God Who works in you what is good. How? He has so constituted you that, when you act with wisdom and discretion, you feel Him in your reason. For the irrational animal does all its deeds without intellect or wisdom, without discretion or shame; it does not know God, being irrational, though it feels Him, being His creature. But the rational animal, which is Man, has intellect and wisdom, discretion and shame, and does rational deeds, which is the first root fixed by God's grace in every person given life and soul. These powers flourish where there is reason, for all of them make people know God, so that they may choose what is just. Therefore, the deed that a person embraces in his Savior, the Son of God through Whom the Father does His works in the Holy Spirit, is productive and perfect and prosperous; and the fiery grace of Christ Jesus calls this to the person's mind and kindles his enthusiasm anew.

Beatrice of Nazareth (1200–1268)

Many of the biographical details handed down about Beatrice of Nazareth's early life contradict each other. Yet it seems certain she was born in the first few years of the thirteenth century, daughter of Barthelmy (or Bartholomew) De Vleeschouwer. It is said her mother taught her to read Latin using the psalter, but her mother died when she was seven. At the age of eight or nine, she was apparently sent to the Beguines at Leau (Zoutleeuw) and later to the Cistercian convent at Florival. There, at the age of fifteen, she asked to be admitted to the Cistercian order, and her persistent pleading led to her acceptance and profession one year later on Pentecost, 1216. Her father, her brother, and two or three of her sisters each became Cistercians as well, possibly professed with her in 1216. Shortly thereafter she was sent to LaRamee to learn manuscript copying, and it was there she began a strong spiritual friendship with Ida of Nivelles. She lived at three Cistercian houses founded by her father, at Florival, Val-des-Vierges, and Nazareth, and spent the last thirty years of her life as abbess at Nazareth, where she died on August 29, 1268.

The text of "The Seven Steps of Love" was dictated by her in Old Flemish to her confessor who, after she died, translated it into Latin at the request of her community. It is characteristic of Beguine spirituality of the thirteenth century. The steps, which she briefly presents, are as follows. (1) The desire to serve God comes wholly from love, and the soul examines its motives and with urgency seeks what can draw it to deeper love. (2) At the second level, the soul seeks to serve God from love alone, and has no other motive, wishing only to please the Lord. (3) The third level finds the soul in torment because it is not able to do enough, give enough, love enough. It knows that fulfillment is beyond human strength, yet it still suffers from fear that its total surrender is not sufficient. (4) The fourth level produces both delight and suffering. There is a clarity and a closeness to God, and the soul is wholly filled with love, so much so that it sometimes cannot control the body. (5) At the fifth level, further demands are made on the soul and by the soul, because of a great crashing of desire and love, which is stirred up like a great storm, and the more the soul is given from above, the more it demands. (6) This next level is even more intimate, and the soul is in command and wholly free. It understands itself as completely in love with God and cannot be stirred by evil, it having been granted free conscience, sweetness of heart, and good judgment. (7) The seventh and highest level the soul attains on this earth finds the soul drawn well beyond human understanding, submerged in love, both exalted and humbled, soothed and later tortured. It recognizes the earth as a long exile and experiences a passionate longing for Christ, as it recognizes it must love in hope. Yet it knows that all obstacles will be removed and that it will eventually hold and be held by the everlasting Godhead.

Love without Return

And there is another manner of loving, which is when the soul seeks to serve our Lord for nothing in return, for love alone, without demanding to know the reason why and without any reward of grace or glory; just as the lady serves her lord for the sake of her love without any thought of reward, for whom simply to serve him is enough and that he should allow her to serve him. In the same way she desires to serve love and love beyond measure and beyond all human reason with all her deeds of fidelity.

And when this comes upon her, then she is so consumed with desire, so ready to perform any service, so cheerful in toil, so gentle in tribulation, so light-hearted in sadness, and she desires with all her being to serve him. And so it is her delight when she finds something she can do or endure in the service of love and in its honour.

The Power of Love

Sometimes it happens that love is sweetly awoken in the soul and joyfully arises and moves in the heart of itself without us doing anything at all. And then the heart is so powerfully touched by love, so keenly drawn into love and so strongly seized by love, and so utterly mastered by love and so tenderly embraced by love that it entirely yields itself to love. And in this it experiences a great proximity to God, a spiritual radiance, a marvellous bliss, a noble freedom, an ecstatic sweetness, a great overpowering by the strength of love, and an overflowing abundance of immense delight. And then she feels that all her senses are sanctified by love and her will has become love, and that she is so deeply immersed and so engulfed in the abyss of love that she herself has turned entirely into love. Then the beauty of love has bedecked her, the power of love has devoured her, the sweetness of love has submerged her, the grandeur of love has consumed her, the nobility of love has enveloped her, the purity of love has adorned her, and the sublimity of love has drawn her upwards and so united herself with her that she always must be love and do nothing but the deeds of love.

The Goad of Love

For the more the soul is given from above, the more she desires, and the more that is revealed to her, the more she is seized by a desire to draw near to the light of truth, of purity, of sanctity and of love's delight. And thus she is driven and goaded on more and more and knows no peace or satisfaction; for the very thing that tortures her and gives her the greatest suffering, makes her whole, and what wounds her most deeply, is the source of her greatest relief.

The Vision of Love

Therefore the soul always wills to follow love, to know love and to delight in love. But she cannot do so in this exile. And so she

desires to return to her homeland where she has already made
her dwelling and to which she turns with all her will and where
she will finally rest in love. For this she knows well: there, all
obstacles will be removed from her and she will be received in
love by Love.

And there she will eagerly look upon him whom she has loved
so tenderly and shall possess him for her eternal good whom she
has so faithfully served. And she will enjoy him in the fullness
of delight whom she has embraced so often in her soul with
love . . . .

There the soul is united with her bridegroom and becomes one
spirit with him in indivisible love and eternal fidelity. And the
soul who strove her utmost in the time of grace shall savour him
in everlasting glory, when praise and love shall be all our work.

Gertrude the Great (1256–1302)

Gertrude went to the nuns at Helfta in Germany at the age of five. Nearly four hundred years later the Pope directed her feast be observed throughout the Church on November 16, but she was never formally canonized. She was friend and pupil of the visionary mystic Mechtild of Magdeburg (1210–1297), who also lived at Helfta.

Little is known of her parentage or the circumstances which led to her being placed in the famous Helfta convent, where she learned Latin and worked copying manuscripts, living the Rule of St. Benedict. Gertrude's mystical visions began in her early twenties, her age at this time is variously placed at twenty-five or twenty-six, and her devotion to the Sacred Heart of Jesus draws on her recognizing the heart of Jesus as the bond and bridge between his humanity and his divinity. Like her sister mystics at the Helfta monastery, Gertrude was well-educated, specifically in the theological sciences. Her *Revelations* are from her own hand and from her notes.

The selections here point out her understanding of the soul's relationship with God in prayer, a delicate subject which she treats forthrightly. The first selection points out how, when we recognize the problems within ourselves, we are able to ask God for their healing. She shows us God as mother, pointing out that a mother more easily and lovingly can look at the child opposite her than on those beside her. In the second selection she teaches the healthy point that no matter what sorrow afflicts a person, prayer for others, and consideration of their difficulties, will assuage and heal personal pain and trials. Next she points out that humble recognition of our own problems will lead us to ask for the prayers of others.

The external effort and result of prayer, the working with and for other persons, should be full of a correct zeal, which she says is marked by charity, discretion, and an understanding that everything one does is for the glory of God. In the final selection she relates her knowledge of the virtue of patience, that prayers are answered when and as they should be.

From the Revelations of St. Gertrude

Chapter LX
That God is pleased with us when we are displeased with ourselves.

As Gertrude prayed for a person with special affection, and said to our Lord, "Hear me, O loving Lord, according to the sweetness of Thy paternal love, for her for whom I pray,"—our Lord answered: "I usually hear when you pray for her." "Why, then," replied Gertrude, "does she so often entreat me to pray for her, alleging always her unworthiness and nothingness, as if she never received any consolation from Thee?" "This," answered the Savior, "is the sweetest way in which My spouse could gain My affection; this ornament becomes her best, and in this she pleases Me most, because thus she is displeasing to herself and this grace increases in her in proportion as you pray for her." On another occasion, when she prayed at the same time for this person and also for another, our Lord said to her: "I have brought her nearer to Me, and therefore it is necessary she should be purified by some little trial; even as a young girl who, on account of her love and tenderness for her mother, wishes to seat herself beside her, although she may be more inconvenienced thereby than her sisters, who take their proper seats round their mother, the mother also cannot look so easily and lovingly on the child beside her as on those who sit opposite to her."

Chapter LXI
Of the effect of prayers for others.

As Gertrude once prostrated at the feet of our Lord Jesus, and kissed His Wounds with all possible respect and devotion, before praying for several persons and several affairs which had been recommended to her, she saw a stream breaking forth from the Heart of Jesus, which appeared to water all the place where she was. She understood that this stream was the efficacy of the prayers which she had offered at His feet, and said to Him: "My Lord, what advantage will these persons receive for whom I have prayed, since they cannot feel the effect of my prayers, and consequently cannot expect any consolation therefrom?" Our Lord answered by the following similitude: "When a king makes peace after a long war, those who live at a distance cannot be made aware of it until a favorable opportunity occurs; thus they who separate themselves from Me by their diffidence or other defects cannot perceive when others pray for them." "But, Lord," she replied, "Thou hast Thyself made known to me that some of those for whom I have prayed are not separated far from Thee." "It is true," answered our Lord; "but he to whom the king gives his orders personally, and not through his officers, must wait for the convenience of his prince. And thus I will Myself make known to them the effect of your prayers, when I find it will be most advantageous to them to do so."

Gertrude then prayed specially for a person who had persecuted her formerly, and received this reply: "As it would be impossible for any one to have his foot pierced through without his heart sympathizing in its sufferings, so My paternal goodness cannot fail to look with eyes of mercy on those who, while they groan under their own infirmaties and feel their need of pardon, are nevertheless moved by holy charity to pray for the welfare of their neighbor."

Of the value and importance of recommending ourselves to the prayers of others.

As the Saint prayed for a person who had requested her prayers with great humility, both personally and through others, she saw our Lord approach this person, encompassing her with celestial light, and pouring forth on her in the midst of this splendor all the graces which she had hoped to receive through the merits of the prayers of Gertrude. Our Lord taught her by this, that when anyone confides in the prayers of another, with a firm confidence that through their intercession they will receive grace from God, the Lord in His goodness pours forth His benedictions on them according to the measure of their desires and their faith, even when he to whose prayers they have recommended themselves neglects to pray for them.

Chapter LXVII
Of the right manner of exercising zeal.

As Gertrude prayed for a person whose conscience was troubled, fearing that she was guilty before God for not having borne with sufficient patience the negligence of some persons by whose bad example she feared religious discipline would become relaxed, our Lord, who is the best of all masters, instructed her thus: "If any one desires that her zeal should be an acceptable sacrifice to Me, and useful to her own soul, she should have a special care of three things; first, she should show a gentle and serene countenance towards those whom she desires to correct for their faults, and even, when opportunity offers, she should manifest her charity towards them by her actions as well as by her words; secondly, she should be careful not to publish these negligences in places where she neither expects amendment in the person corrected nor caution in the listeners; thirdly, when her conscience urges her to reprehend any fault, no human consideration should induce her to be silent, but, from a pure motive of giving glory to God and benefiting souls, let her seek an opportunity of correcting these imperfections with profit and charity. Then she will be rewarded according to her labor, not according to her success; for if her care entirely fails of effect, it will not be her fault, but the fault of those who refuse to hear her."

As the Saint prayed again for two persons who had a verbal disagreement, one anxious for the maintenance of justice, and the other for charity, our Lord said to her: "When a father who loves his little children sees them playing together and disporting merely for amusement, he appears not to notice it; but if he perceives that one rises up against the other too harshly, then he immediately reprehends severely the one who is in fault. Thus also I, who am the Father of mercies, when I see two persons arguing together with a good intention, appear not to perceive it, though I would much prefer to see them enjoy an entire peace of heart; but if one becomes angry with the other, she shall not escape the rod of My paternal justice."

Chapter LXVIII
That we do not always receive the fruit of our prayers immediately.

As another person complained that she did not receive the fruit of the prayers which were offered for her, the Saint laid the matter before God, and received this reply: "Ask this person what she would think most advantageous to a cousin or any other relative for whom she ardently desired a benefice,—whether the right to it should be conferred on him as a child, or whether he should be allowed the revenues also and permitted to use them as he pleased? According to human prudence, she could only reply that it would be more advantageous to confer on him the right to the benefice, and the revenue when he could use it properly, than when he might squander it wastefully. Let her, then, confide in My wisdom and My Divine mercy, since I am her Father, her Brother, and her Spouse, and I will obtain what will be advantageous for her body and soul with far more care and fidelity than she would for any relative; and let her believe that I preserve carefully the fruit of all the prayers and desires which are addressed to Me for her, until a suitable time comes to permit her the enjoyment of them; then I will commit them to her entirely, when no one will be able to corrupt them, or to deprive her of them by their importunities. And let her be persuaded that this is far more useful to her than to pour into her soul some sweetness which might, perhaps, be an occasion of vainglory to her, or become tarnished by her pride; or than to grant her some temporal prosperity, which might prove an occasion of sin."

Julian of Norwich (1342–1423)

Julian of Norwich is the unknown anchorite who entered her anchorhold, at the Church of St. Julian in Conisford at Norwich, when she was about thirty. She was one of a number of medieval women mystics, and, despite her *pro forma* protestations of lack of education, her writings present her as among the best educated. Her youthful prayer asked that she participate in the passion as one who loved Christ, to suffer with Him both spiritual and physical pain, and to be given three wounds: contrition, compassion, and longing for God.

Julian's first visionary experience quite probably occurred before she enclosed herself. During an illness she had such a striking vision of the suffering of Jesus that her own mother thought her dead. She wrote of these visions, calling them revelations or showings, soon after they occurred, probably in the early 1370s. After years of prayer she began to understand more about these visions, and she returned to the text in 1393.

Many came to her anchorhold to seek spiritual counsel, including Margery Kempe of Lynne, who wrote of a unique way to follow Christ through contemplation, active works, and pilgrimage. Julian's insight into the workings of the soul confirmed the spiritual nature of Margery's often uncontrollable emotional responses to the Lord.

Her narration of visions is much like that of Hildegard of Bingen, but her later writing shows a theological sophistication far surpassing that of her predecessors and contemporaries. She is known to students of spirituality for her understanding of the motherhood of God and particularly for her presentation of Jesus as mother: "To the property of motherhood belong nature, love, wisdom, and knowledge, and this is God" (chapter 60). Those versed in contemporary literature recognize her recurring theme of trust in God from T. S. Eliot's *Four Quartets*: "And all shall be well and/All manner of thing shall be well/By the purification of the motive/In the ground of our beseeching" ("Little Gidding"). It is the second theme that most of the following selections from the long text take up.

The first selection initially refers to her vision of the suffering Jesus. God shows her the hazelnut, able to fall into nothingness but cared for and known insofar as it attaches itself to God.

The second shows God telling her that sin is necessary, but all shall be well, and continues her understanding of the passion.

In the third God again says that all shall be well, and tells the soul he takes heed of everything that happens, and that even the worst things can turn out to be from the hand of God.

The last selection tells of God wanting us to know three things about prayer: that prayer originates in and from God, that all prayer should be turned toward the will of God, and that the fruit and end of our prayer is to be united to God in love. God teaches us that our trust must be equal to our prayer, so that it will overcome both our weaknesses and our fears.

The Fifth Chapter

At the same time as I saw this sight of the head bleeding, our good Lord showed a spiritual sight of his familiar love. I saw that he is to us everything which is good and comforting for our help. He is our clothing, who wraps and enfolds us for love, embraces us and shelters us, surrounds us for his love, which is so tender that he may never desert us. And so in this sight I saw that he is everything which is good, as I understand.

And in this he showed me something small, no bigger than a hazelnut, lying in the palm of my hand, as it seemed to me, and it was as round as a ball. I looked at it with the eye of my understanding and thought: What can this be? I was amazed that it could last, for I thought that because of its littleness it would suddenly have fallen into nothing. And I was answered in my understanding: It lasts and always will, because God loves it; and thus everything has being through the love of God.

In this little thing I saw three properties. The first is that God made it, the second is that God loves it, the third is that God preserves it. But what did I see in it? It is that God is the Creator and the protector and the lover. For until I am substantially united to him, I can never have perfect rest or true happiness, until, that is, I am so attached to him that there can be no created thing between my God and me.

This little thing which is created seemed to me as if it could have fallen into nothing because of its littleness. We need to have knowledge of this, so that we may delight in despising as nothing everything created, so as to love and have uncreated God. For this is the reason why our hearts and souls are not in perfect ease, because here we seek rest in this thing which is so little, in which there is no rest, and we do not know our God who is almighty, all wise and all good, for he is true rest. God wishes to be known, and it pleases him that we should rest in him; for everything which is beneath him is not sufficient for us. And this is the reason why no soul is at rest until it has despised as nothing all things which are created. When it by its will has become nothing for love, to have him who is everything, then it is able to receive spiritual rest.

And also our good Lord revealed that it is very greatly pleasing to him that a simple soul should come naked, openly and familiarly. For this is the loving yearning of the soul through the touch of the Holy Spirit, from the understanding which I have in this revelation: God, of your goodness give me yourself, for you are enough for me, and I can ask for nothing which is less which can pay you full worship. And if I ask anything which is less, always I am in want; but only in you do I have everything.

And these words of the goodness of God are very dear to the soul, and very close to touching our Lord's will, for his goodness fills all his creatures and all his blessed works full, and endlessly overflows in them. For he is everlastingness, and he made us only for himself, and restored us by his precious Passion and always preserves us in his blessed love, and all this is of his goodness.

The Twenty-Seventh Chapter

And after this our Lord brought to my mind the longing that I had for him before, and I saw that nothing hindered me but sin, and I saw that this is true of us all in general, and it seemed to me that if there had been no sin, we should all have been pure and as like our Lord as he created us. And so in my folly before this time I often wondered why, through the great prescient wisdom of God, the beginning of sin was not prevented. For then it seemed to me that all would have been well.

The impulse to think this was greatly to be shunned; and nevertheless I mourned and sorrowed on this account, unreasonably, lacking discretion. But Jesus, who in this vision informed me about everything needful to me, answered with these words and said: Sin is necessary, but all will be well, and all will be well, and every kind of thing will be well. In this naked word 'sin', our Lord brought generally to my mind all which is not good, and the shameful contempt and the direst tribulation which he endured for us in this life, and his death and all his pains, and the passions, spiritual and bodily, of all his creatures. For we are all in part troubled, and we shall be troubled, following our master Jesus until we are fully purged of our mortal flesh and all our inward affections which are not very good.

And with the beholding of this, with all the pains that ever were or will be, I understood Christ's Passion for the greatest and surpassing pain. And yet this was shown to me in an instant, and it quickly turned into consolation. For our good Lord would not have the soul frightened by this ugly sight. But I did not see sin, for I believe that it has no kind of substance, no share in being, nor can it be recognized except by the pain caused by it. And it seems to me that this pain is something for a time, for it purges and makes us know ourselves and ask for mercy; for the Passion of our Lord is comfort to us against all this, and that is his blessed will. And because of the tender love which our good Lord has for all who will be saved, he comforts readily and sweetly, meaning this: It is true that sin is the cause of all this pain, but all will be well, and every kind of thing will be well.

These words were revealed most tenderly, showing no kind of blame to me or to anyone who will be saved. So it would be most unkind of me to blame God or marvel at him on account of my sins, since he does not blame me for sin.

And in these same words I saw hidden in God an exalted and wonderful mystery, which he will make plain and we shall know in heaven. In this knowledge we shall truly see the cause why he allowed sin to come, and in this sight we shall rejoice forever.

The Thirty-Second Chapter

On one occasion our Good Lord said: Every kind of thing will be well; and on another occasion he said: You will see yourself that every kind of thing will be well. And from these two the soul gained different kinds of understanding. One was this: that he wants us to know that he takes heed not only of things which are noble and great, but also of those which are little and small, of humble men and simple, of this man and that man. And this is what he means when he says: Every kind of thing will be well. For he wants us to know that the smallest thing will not be forgotten. Another understanding is this: that there are many deeds which in our eyes are so evilly done and lead to such great harms that it seems to us impossible that any good result could ever come of them. And we contemplate this and sorrow and mourn for it so that we cannot rest in the blessed contemplation of God as we ought to do. And the cause is this: that the reason which we use is now so blind, so abject and so stupid that we cannot recognize God's exalted, wonderful wisdom, or the power and the goodness of the blessed Trinity. And this is his intention when he says: You will see yourself that every kind of thing will be well, as if he said: Accept it now in faith and trust, and in the very end you will see truly, in fullness of joy.

And so in the same five words said before: I may make all things well, I understand a powerful comfort from all the works of our Lord God which are still to come.

There is a deed which the blessed Trinity will perform on the last day, as I see it, and what the deed will be and how it will be performed is unknown to every creature who is inferior to

Christ, and it will be until the deed is done. The goodness and the love of our Lord God want us to know that this will be, and his power and his wisdom, through the same love, want to conceal it and hide it from us, what it will be and how it will be done. And the cause why he wants us to know it like this is because he wants us to be at ease with our souls and at peace in love, disregarding every disturbance which could hinder our true rejoicing in him.

This is the great deed ordained by our God from without beginning, treasured and hidden in his blessed breast, known only to himself, through which deed he will make all things well. For just as the blessed Trinity created all things from nothing, just so will the same blessed Trinity make everything well which is not well. And I marvelled greatly at this sight, and contemplated our faith, with this in my mind: Our faith is founded on God's word, and it belongs to our faith that we believe that God's word will be preserved in all things. And one article of our faith is that many creatures will be damned, such as the angels who fell out of heaven because of pride, who now are devils, and many men upon earth who die out of the faith of Holy Church, that is to say those who are pagans and many who have received baptism and who live unchristian lives and so die out of God's love. All these will be eternally condemned to hell, as Holy Church teaches me to believe.

And all this being so, it seemed to me that it was impossible that every kind of thing should be well, as our Lord revealed at this time. And to this I had no other answer as a revelation from our Lord except this: What is impossible to you is not impossible to me. I shall preserve my word in everything, and I shall make everything well. And in this I was taught by the grace of God that I ought to keep myself steadfastly in the faith, as I had understood before, and that at the same time I should stand firm and believe firmly that every kind of thing will be well, as our Lord revealed at that same time. For this is the great deed which our Lord will do, and in this deed he will preserve his word in everything. And he will make well all which is not well. But what the deed will be and how it will be done, there is no creature who is inferior to Christ who knows it, or will know it until it has been done, according to the understanding which I received of our Lord's meaning at this time.

The Forty-Second Chapter

Our Lord wants us to have true understanding, and especially in three things which belong to our prayer.

The first is with whom and how our prayer originates. He reveals with whom when he says: I am the ground; and he reveals how by his goodness, because he says: First it is my will.

As to the second, in what manner and how we should perform our prayers, that is that our will should be turned, rejoicing, into the will of our Lord. And he means this when he says: I make you to wish it.

As to the third, it is that we know the fruit and the end of our prayer, which is to be united and like to our Lord in all things. And with this intention and for this end was all this loving lesson revealed, and he wishes to help us, and he will make it so, as he says himself, blessed may he be.

For this is our Lord's will, that our prayer and our trust be both equally generous. For if we do not trust as much as we pray, we do not pay full honor to our Lord in our prayer, and also we impede and hurt ourselves; and the reason is, as I believe, because we do not truly know that our Lord is the ground from which our prayer springs, and also because we do not know that it is given to us by grace from his love. For if we knew this, it would make us trust to have all we desire from our Lord's gift.

For I am sure that no one asks for mercy and grace with a right intention unless mercy and grace be first given. But sometimes it comes to our mind that we have prayed a long time, and still it seems to us that we do not have what we ask for. But we should not be too depressed on this account, for I am sure, according to our Lord's meaning, that either we are waiting for a better occasion, or more grace, or a better gift. He wants us to have true knowledge in himself that he is being; and in this knowledge he wants our understanding to be founded, with all our powers and all our purpose and all our intention. And he wants us to take our place and our dwelling in this foundation. And he wants us to have understanding, by his own light of grace, of three things which follow.

The first is our noble and excellent making, the second our precious and lovable redemption, the third everything which he has made inferior to us to serve us and which he protects for love of us. So he means as if he said: Behold and see that I have done all this before your prayer, and now you are, and you pray to me. And so he means that it is for us to know that the greatest deeds are done as Holy Church teaches.

And contemplating this with thanksgiving, we ought to pray for the deed which is now being done, that is that he may rule us and guide us to his glory in this life, and bring us to his bliss; and therefore he has done everything. So he means us to see that he does it and to pray for it. For the one is not enough, for if we pray and do not see that he does it, it makes us depressed and doubting; and that is not to his glory. And if we see that he does it and do not pray, we do not do our duty. And it cannot be so, that is to say, it is not so in his sight. But to see that he does it, and at the same time to pray, in this way is he worshipped and we are helped. It is our Lord's will that we pray for everything which he has ordained to do, either in particular or in general. And the joy and the bliss that this is to him, and the thanks and the honor that we shall have for it, this is beyond the understanding of all creatures in this life, as I see it.

For prayer is a right understanding of the fullness of joy which is to come, with true longing and trust. The savoring or seeing of our bliss, to which we are ordained, by nature makes us to long; true understanding and love, with a sweet recollection in our savior, by grace makes us to trust. And in these two operations our Lord constantly regards us, for this is our duty, and his goodness cannot assign any less to us than it is our obligation diligently to perform. And when we do it, still it will seem to us that it is nothing. And this is true. But let us do what we can, and meekly ask mercy and grace, and everything which is lacking in us we shall find in him. And this is what he means when he says: I am the foundation of your beseeching.

And so in these blessed words with the revelation I saw a complete overcoming of all our weakness and all our doubting fears.

Catherine of Siena (1347–1380)

Caterina di Giacomo di Benincasa was born in the small Italian city of Siena, about two hundred kilometers north of Rome, the twenty-fourth of her parents' twenty-five children. When she was seven, she vowed herself to Christ; at fifteen she cut her hair in denial of her parents' plans for her marriage. She became a Third Order Dominican—a Mantellata—in her late teens, and lived in solitude in her small stone room in her father's house where, at nineteen, she experienced a mystical marriage with Christ. It was the practice of the Mantellata to perform works of mercy for the sick and the poor, and at the age of twenty-one Catherine rejoined her family and began her corporal works.

Throughout her Dominican life she received the guidance of Dominican confessor-directors, first Bartolomeo de'Dominici, then Raymond of Capua. Because at that time enclosure was society's preferred way of legitimizing a woman's consecration to God within the Church, Catherine had wanted to disguise herself as a man and take the Dominican habit so as to work as a preacher and reformer of her day. She took instead the habit of a Tertiary. In Raymond of Capua's *Legenda* of her life, written in Latin between 1385 and 1395, he records her conversations with the Lord on the matter. "Remember how you used to plan to put on man's attire and enter the Order of Preachers in foreign parts to labor for the good of souls?" Christ asks. "Why then are you surprised, why are you sad, because I am now drawing you on to the work which you have longed for from your infancy?" She protests that she is a woman, that the world has no use for women like that, that women cannot freely associate in the company of men. The Lord answers: "No thing is impossible with God. . . . With me there is no longer male and female . . . for all stand equal in my sight, and all things are equally in my power to do."

Convinced of God's will in her life, in her late twenties she entered into the contemporary ecclesiastical and political controversies between and among the various Italian city-states. She dictated over four hundred letters in the Sienese dialect and reported *The Dialogue* to Raymond. In addition, there are extant twenty-four of the prayers she recited in ecstacy.

Though she did not learn to read until she was thirty, she well preached the reform of the clergy, influenced Gregory XI's return of the papacy to Rome from Avignon in 1377, and suffered the results of the Great Schism of 1378. The year before she died, Gregory's successor, Urban VI, called her to Rome with the hope that her presence would legitimize his papacy.

Catherine died in Rome at the age of thirty-three, following a long period of illness and fasting. Her body lies beneath the main altar of the Church of Santa Maria sopra Minerva. Her work took root in the Church, which named her a Doctor of the Church some six hundred years after her death.

Her spirituality, as revealed in *The Dialogue*, centers on the humble appropriation of self in relation to God revealed in Christ, and on charity. All good and all wickedness, she relates, come from one's relations with one's neighbors. The life of God one seeks to live comes through the recognition of truth, the truth about oneself, and about God revealed in the world. The section below from *The Dialogue* presents this most clearly: ". . . to attain this union and purity: You must never pass judgment in human terms on anything you see or hear from anyone at all, whether it concerns you or someone else. You must consider only my will for them and for you."

From *The Dialogue*

Truth

98

That soul's hunger and thirst, her sincerity and the longing with which she asked to be able to serve him pleased God eternal. So he looked on her with compassionate mercy and said:

O dearest daughter whom I so love, you who are my bride, rise above yourself and open your mind's eye. Look at me, infinite Goodness, and see my unspeakable love for you and my other servants. And open the sensitive ear of your desire. This is the only way you will see and hear, for the soul who does not have my Truth for the object of her mind's eye can neither hear nor know my truth. Therefore I want you to rise above your senses so that you may more surely know the truth. Then I will satisfy you, for I am pleased with your desire and your questioning. Not that you can increase my pleasure: It is I who make you grow, not you me. But the very pleasure I take in my creation pleases me.

So that soul obeyed. She rose above herself to know the truth about what she had asked. Then God eternal said to her:

So that you may better understand what I am about to tell you, let me begin at the source of the answer: the three lights that come forth from me, the true Light.

The first is an ordinary light in those whose charity is ordinary. (I will repeat what I have already told you about this, that, and many other things even though you have already heard them, so that your meager understanding may better comprehend what I want you to know.) The other two lights belong to those who have risen above the world and are seeking perfection. Beyond this I shall explain what you have asked me to, being more specific about what I have already touched on more broadly.

You know that no one can walk in the way of truth without the light of reason that you draw from me, the true Light, through the eye of your understanding. You must have as well the light of faith, which you possess as my gift from holy baptism unless you have put it out with your sins. In baptism, through the power of my only-begotten Son's blood, you received the form of faith. If you exercise this faith by virtue with the light of reason, reason will in turn be enlightened by faith, and such faith will give you life and lead you in the way of truth. With this light you will reach me, the true Light; without it you would come to darkness.

There are two lights drawn from this [first] light that you must have, and to the two I will add yet a third.

The first is that you must all be enlightened to know the transitory things of this world, that they all pass away like the wind. But you cannot know this well unless you first know your own weakness, how ready that perverse law bound up in your members makes you to rebel against me your Creator. Not that this law can force any one of you to commit the least sin unless you want to, but it certainly does fight against the spirit. Nor did I give this law so that my people should be conquered, but so that they might increase and prove virtue in their souls. For virtue can be proved only by its opposite. Sensuality is the opposite of the spirit, so it is through sensuality that the soul proves the love she has for me her Creator. When does she prove it? When she mounts hatred and contempt against it.

I gave the soul this law also to keep her truly humble. So you see, while I created her in my image and likeness and made her so honorable and beautiful, I gave her as well the vilest thing there is, this perverse law. In other words, I bound her into a body formed from the vilest earth so that when she saw her beauty she would not lift up her head in pride against me. So the weak body is a reason for humility to those who have this light [of mine]. They have no reason at all to be proud, but they do have reason for true and perfect humility. This perverse law, then, no matter how it fights, cannot force the least sin. Rather it is reason for you to learn to know yourself and to know how inconstant is the world.

The eye of understanding ought to see this through the light of holy faith, which is that eye's pupil. This is that essential light which everyone in every situation must have to share in the life of grace, in the fruit of the spotless Lamb's blood. This is the ordinary light, and everyone must have it. Those who do not have it are damned. Because they do not have the light they are not living in grace, for without the light they do not recognize the evil of sin or its cause, so they cannot shun its cause or hate it.

Likewise, those who do not recognize good and the cause of good, that is, virtue, can neither love nor desire me, Goodness itself, or the virtue I have given you as a means and instrument of grace from me, the true Good.

So you see how much you need this light, for your sin consists simply in loving what I hate and hating what I love. I love virtue and I hate vice. So whoever loves vice and hates virtue offends me and loses my grace. Such people behave as if they were blind. Not recognizing the cause of vice, sensual selfishness, they have neither contempt for themselves nor knowledge of vice and the evil vice brings upon them. Nor do they know virtue or me, the Source of life-giving virtue, or the dignity they should preserve in themselves by coming to grace through virtue.

So you see, lack of knowledge is the cause of their evil. How necessary it is, then, for you to have this light!

99

But once the soul has gained this ordinary light she ought not rest content. For as long as you are pilgrims in this life you are capable of growing and should grow. Those who are not growing are by that very fact going backward. Either you should be growing in that ordinary light that you have gained with the help of my grace, or you should be making a genuine effort to advance to the second and more perfect light, to rise from the imperfect to the perfect. For the light gives the soul the will to advance to perfection.

In this second light there are two sorts of perfect souls. The perfect are those who have risen above the ordinary worldly way of living, and there are two sorts. The first are those who give themselves perfectly to punishing their bodies by performing severe and enormous penances. To keep their sensuality from rebelling against reason, these have all set their object more in mortifying their bodies than in slaying their selfish wills. They feed at the table of penance, and they are good and perfect if their penance has its root in me and is guided by the light of discernment. In other words, they must truly know themselves and me, be very humble, and be wholly subject to the judgments of my will rather than to those of other people.

But if they are not thus truly and humbly clothed in my will, they may often sin against their very perfection by setting themselves up as judges over those whose way is not the same as theirs. Do you know why this happens? Because they have invested more effort and desire in mortifying their bodies than in slaying their selfish wills. They are always wanting to choose times and places and spiritual consolations in their own way, and even earthly troubles and conflict with the devil (the way I told you about in the second, imperfect stage). They are their very own deceivers, deceived by that selfish will that I have called "spiritual self-will," and in their self-delusion they say: "I would like to have this consolation rather than this conflict or trouble with the devil. Nor is it for myself that I say this, but to be more pleasing to God and to have more grace in my soul. For it seems to me I could serve and possess him better in this way than in that."

In this way they often fall into suffering and weariness, and so become insupportable to themselves and sin against their very perfection. And they are not even aware that they are lying there in the filth of their pride. But there they lie. For if it were not so, if they were truly humble and not presumptuous, they would see by the light that I, gentle first Truth, name the situation, the time, and the place, consolations or trials, whatever is necessary for salvation and to bring souls to the perfection for which I chose them. And they would see that everything I give is for love, and that therefore they should accept everything with love and reverence. This is what the others do, those who reach the third stage, as I shall tell you. These two sorts of people both live in this most perfect light.

100

Those who reach the third stage (which follows after the other) are perfect in every situation once they have come into this glorious light. No matter what I send them, they hold it in due reverence, as I mentioned when I spoke to you about the third and unitive stages of the soul. They consider themselves deserving of sufferings and outrages from the world, worthy to be deprived of any consolation at all that may be theirs. And just as they consider themselves deserving of suffering, so they also count themselves unworthy of any fruit that may come to them from their suffering. These have known and tasted in the light my eternal will, which wants only your good and permits you these things so that you may be made holy in me.

After the soul has come to know my will she clothes herself in it and attends only to how she may keep and intensify her perfection for the glory and praise of my name. In the light of faith she fixes her mind's eye on Christ crucified, my only-begotten Son, loving and following his teaching, which is rule and way for the perfect and imperfect alike. She sees how the Lamb my Truth is in love with her and instructs her in perfection, and seeing it, she falls in love with him. Perfection is what she came to know when she saw this gentle loving Word, my only-begotten Son, finding his nourishment at the table of holy desire by seeking honor for me his eternal Father and salvation for you. In this desire he ran eagerly to his shameful death on the cross and fulfilled the obedience that I his Father had laid on him. He did not shun toil or shame, did not hold back because of your ingratitude and foolish failure to recognize the great favor he had done you. The hounding of the Jews could not hold him back, nor the jeering insults and grumbling, nor the shouts of the people. He went through it all like a true knight and captain whom I had put on the battlefield to wrest you from the devils' hands. He freed you from the most perverse slavery there could be. This is why he instructed you in his way, his teaching, his rule. And this is why you can approach the gate to me, eternal Life, with the key of his precious blood that was poured out with such burning love, with hatred and contempt for your sins.

It is as if this gentle loving Word, my Son, were saying to you: "Look. I have made the road and opened the gate for you with my blood. Do not fail, then, to follow it. Do not sit down to rest out of selfish concern for yourself, foolishly saying you do not know the way. Do not presume to choose your way of serving instead of the one I have made for you in my own person, eternal Truth, incarnate Word, the straight way hammered out with my own blood."

Get up, then, and follow him, for no one can come to me the Father except through him. He is the way and the gate through whom you must enter into me, the sea of peace.

When the soul, then, has come to taste this light after so delightfully seeing and knowing it, she runs to the table of holy desire, in love as she is and eager with a lover's restlessness. She has no eyes for herself, for seeking her own spiritual or material comfort. Rather, as one who has completely drowned her own will in this light and knowledge, she shuns no burden, from whatever source it may come. She even endures the pain of shame and vexations from the devil and other people's grumbling, feasting at the table of the most holy cross on honor for me, God eternal, and salvation for others.

She seeks no recompense either from me or from others, because she is stripped of any mercenary love, of any loving me for her own profit. She is clothed in perfect light, and loves me sincerely without any other concern than the glory and praise of my name. She does not serve me for her own pleasure or her neighbors for her own profit, but only for love.

Souls such as these have let go of themselves, have stripped off their old nature, their selfish sensuality, and clothed themselves in a new nature, the gentle Christ Jesus, my Truth, and they follow him courageously. These are they who have sat down at the table of holy desire, and have set their minds more on slaying their selfish will than on mortifying and killing their bodies. They have, it is true, mortified their bodies, but not as their chief concern. Rather, they have used mortification as the instrument it is to help them slay their self-will. (I told you this when I was explaining my statement that I would have few words and many deeds.) And this is what you should do. Your chief desire ought to be to slay your selfish will so that it neither seeks nor wants anything but to follow my gentle Truth, Christ crucified, by seeking the honor and glory of my name and the salvation of souls.

Those who live in this gentle light do just this. Therefore they are always peaceful and calm, and nothing can scandalize them because they have done away with what causes them to take scandal, their self-will. They trample underfoot all the persecutions the world and the devil can hound them with. They can stand in the water of great troubles and temptations, but it cannot hurt them because they are anchored to the vine of burning desire.

They find joy in everything. They do not sit in judgment on my servants or anyone else, but rejoice in every situation and every way of living they see, saying, "Thanks to you, eternal

Father, that in your house there are so many dwelling places!"
And they are happier to see many different ways than if they were
to see everyone walking the same way, because this way they see
the greatness of my goodness more fully revealed. In everything
they find joy and the fragrance of the rose. This is true not only
of good things; even when they see something that is clearly sin-
ful they do not pass judgment, but rather feel a holy and genuine
compassion, praying for the sinner and saying with perfect humility, "Today it is your turn; tomorrow it will be mine unless
divine grace holds me up."

O dearest daughter, let the love of this sweet marvelous state
take hold of you. Look at those who run along in this glorious
light and their own magnificence. Their spirits are holy and they
feast at the table of holy desire. By this light they have come to
find their nourishment in the food of souls for the honor of me
the eternal Father. They are clothed in the lovely garment, the
teaching, of the Lamb, my only-begotten Son, with flaming
charity.

They do not waste their time passing false judgment, either
against my servants or the world's servants. They are not scandalized by any grumbling on anyone's part: if it is against themselves they are happy to suffer for my name, and when it is against
someone else they bear with it in compassion for their neighbor,
grumbling neither against the grumbler nor the victim, because
their love for me and for their neighbor is well ordered. And because their love is well ordered, dearest daughter, they are never
scandalized in those they love, nor in any person, because in this
regard they are blind, and therefore they assume no right to be
concerned with the intentions of other people but only with dis-
cerning my merciful will.

They are faithful to the teaching that you know my Truth gave
you early in your life when you asked with great longing to be
led to perfect purity. You know that when you were wondering
how you might attain this, your desire was answered while you
were asleep. The voice sounded not only in your mind but in your
ear as well—so much so, if you recall, that you returned to your
bodily senses when my Truth spoke thus to you:

"Do you wish to reach perfect purity and be so freed from scandal that your spirit will not take scandal in anything at all? Then
see that you remain united with me in loving affection, for I am

supreme and eternal purity. I am the fire that purifies the soul. So the nearer the soul comes to me the more pure she will become, and the more she departs from me the more unclean she is. This is why worldly folk fall into such wickedness, because they have left me. But the soul who unites herself directly with me shares in my own purity.

"There is another thing you must do to attain this union and purity: You must never pass judgment in human terms on anything you see or hear from anyone at all, whether it concerns you or someone else. You must consider only my will for them and for you.

"And if you should see something that is clearly a sin or fault, snatch the rose from that thorn. In other words, offer these things to me in holy compassion. As for any assault against yourself, consider that my will permits it to prove virtue in you and in my other servants. And assume that the offender does such a thing as an instrument commissioned by me. For often such a person's intention is good; there is no one who can judge the hidden heart.

"When you cannot see clearly and openly whether the sin is deadly, you must not pass judgment in your mind, but be concerned only about my will for that person. And if you do see it, you must respond not with judgment but with holy compassion. In this way you will attain perfect purity, for if you act this way your spirit will not be scandalized either in me or in your neighbors. For you cast contempt on your neighbors when you pay attention to their ill will toward you rather than my will for them. Such contempt and scandal alienates the soul from me, blocks her perfection, and to some extent deprives her of grace—in proportion to the seriousness of the contempt and hatred she has conceived for her neighbor because of her judgmental thoughts.

"Things go just the opposite for the soul who is concerned for my will. For I will only your well-being, and whatever I give, I give it so that you may reach the goal for which I created you. The soul who considers things in this light remains always in love for her neighbors, and so she remains in my love. And because she remains in my love she remains united with me.

"So if you would attain the purity you ask of me, there are three principal things you must do. You must be united with me in loving affection, bearing in your memory the blessings you have received from me. With the eye of your understanding you must see my affectionate charity, how unspeakably much I love you. And where the human will is concerned you must consider my will rather than people's evil intentions, for I am their judge—not you, but I. If you do this, all perfection will be yours."

This, if you remember well, was the teaching my Truth gave you.

Now I tell you, dearest daughter, those who have learned this teaching taste the pledge of eternal life even in this life. If you keep this teaching in mind you will fall neither into the devil's trap (for you will recognize it) nor into the traps you asked me about. Still, to satisfy your desire I will tell you more clearly how you may never think judgmentally but only in holy compassion.

Teresa of Avila (1515–1582)

When Teresa de Ahumada was fourteen her mother died, and her father sent her to be educated at a convent in their small, walled city, Avila, Spain. There she came under the influence of a nun who convinced her of the wonders of God. She also spoke with Dona Juana Suarez at the Carmelite Convent of the Incarnation just outside Avila who, she attests, convinced her that her vocation lay within that Carmel.

During this time of decision she became seriously ill and returned to her father's house. Once recovered, she went to visit her married sister, but she stayed a while visiting her father's brother, the friar Don Pedro. He asked her to read his religious books to him, which she did. While Teresa had not yet decided to become a nun, she began to believe religious life would be her most certain path to salvation, and she decided to force herself to embrace it. As she recounted in her *Autobiography*, her conflict lasted three months, during which she determined that however purgatorial the religious life might be, it would serve to grant her heaven. This decision, "inspired by servile fear more than by love," was opposed by her father.

Teresa entered the Avila Carmel at age twenty. She wrote that she had no love of God to supplant the love for her father and relatives, "But the Lord gave me courage to fight against myself and so I carried out my intention." She apparently took the habit at the Convent of the Incarnation on November 2, 1536, and made her solemn profession one year later. "When I took the habit, the Lord at once showed me how great are His favors to those who use force with themselves in His service," and she found a new joy to her life.

It is generally understood that this Carmel was a relatively frivolous place, but current scholarship argues that extreme poverty caused its many inhabitants to lead busy lives. Novices, including Teresa, were not educated to mental prayer. There was little in the way of recollection, and Teresa recounts the superficiality of her interior life and discouragement at her desolation until she was granted the grace of complete surrender at about the age of forty. The changes within her did not match her uncontemplative surroundings, and she eventually received permission to found another Carmel in Avila with four postulants in 1562. Five years later she received permission to start as many houses as she could, and so began her career as a traveling contemplative.

She is best known for her instructions on prayer and for her commentary on the Lord's prayer in *The Way of Perfection*. Her recommendations in *The Foundations*, which includes as well a narrative of her founding of Carmelite convents, are fresh with insight today: "If [obedience] sends you to the kitchen, remember that the Lord walks among the pots and pans." Teresa's major works are complemented by her minor works, including *Meditations on the Canticle* (Song of Songs) and *Visitation of the Discalced Nuns*.

The Interior Castle, from which the selection below is taken, is her most complete treatise on the interior life. The King resides at the center of seven crystal mansions, and only he can guide the soul to himself. Each mansion has several rooms, and her work depicts the soul moving through many, but not all of them, to meet the King at their center. Each mansion is a step in the spiritual life. The first three focus on meditative prayer, pious reading, and the practice of love. The fourth introduces the prayer of quiet, where the Lord invites the soul to move to a contemplative life with him. The fifth and sixth further describe the state

of infused contemplation, and in the sixth mansion she specifically recommends intuitive meditation on the humanity
of Christ. It is in the seventh mansion that the soul experiences the mystical marriage with Christ.

The sections from the third and fourth mansions, below,
present total surrender to the will of God as the key to union
with Him in prayer and in love, as well as the understanding that it is we who need to recognize our faults and ask
for their healing before we attempt to criticize others.
Toward this end she recommends "someone to consult" so
that the individual will more readily be able to recognize
the will of God and be able "to bear the trial that would
come from their zeal."

Teresa of Jesus was canonized by Pope Gregory XV in
1622, and proclaimed the first woman doctor of the Church
on September 27, 1970. Her feast is celebrated by the universal Church on October 15.

From *The Interior Castle*

The Third Dwelling Places

Chapter Two

10. It will seem to you that consolations and spiritual delights
are the same, so why should I make this distinction? To me it
seems there is a very great difference between the two. Now I can
be wrong. I'll say what I understand about this when I speak of
the fourth dwelling places, which come after these. For since something will have to be explained about the spiritual delights the
Lord gives there, the discussion will be more appropriate at that
time. And although the explanation may seem to be useless it
might help somewhat so that in understanding the nature of each
thing you will be able to strive for what is best. Great solace comes
to souls God brings there, and confusion to those who think they
have everything. If souls are humble they will be moved to give
thanks. If there is some lack in humility, they will feel an inner
distaste for which they will find no reason. For perfection as well
as its reward does not consist in spiritual delights but in greater
love and in deeds done with greater justice and truth.

11. . . . when I read in books about these delights and favors the Lord grants souls that serve Him, I was very much consoled and moved to give great praise to God. Well, if my soul, which was so wretched, did this, those souls that are good and humble will praise Him much more. And if one alone is led to praise Him even once, it is in my opinion very good that the subject be mentioned so that we know about the happiness and delight we lose through our own fault. Moreover, if these favors are from God they come brimming over with love and fortitude by which you can journey with less labor and grow in the practice of works and virtues. Don't think that it matters little to lose such favors through our own fault; when it isn't our fault, the Lord is just. His Majesty will give you through other paths what He keeps from you on this one because of what He knows, for His secrets are very hidden; at least what He does will without any doubt be what is most suitable for us.

12. What it seems to me would be highly beneficial for those who through the goodness of the Lord are in this state (for, as I have said, He grants them no small mercy because they are very close to ascending higher) is that they study diligently how to be prompt in obedience. And even if they are not members of a religious order, it would be a great thing for them to have—as do many persons—someone whom they could consult so as not to do their own will in anything. Doing our own will is usually what harms us. And they shouldn't seek another of their own making, as they say—one who is so circumspect about everything; but seek out someone who is very free from illusion about the things of the world. For in order to know ourselves, it helps a great deal to speak with someone who already knows the world for what it is. And it helps also because when we see some things done by others that seem so impossible for us and the ease with which they do them, it is very encouraging and seems that through their flight we also will make bold to fly, as do the bird's fledglings when they are taught; for even though they do not begin to soar immediately, little by little they imitate the parent. Receiving this help is most beneficial; I know. These persons will be right, however determined they are to keep from offending the Lord, not to place themselves in the occasion of offending Him. . . . The devil knows well how to stir up tempests so as to do us harm,

and these persons would be unable to bear the trials that would come from their zeal to prevent others from committing sin.

13. Let us look at our own faults and leave aside those of others, for it is very characteristic of persons with such well-ordered lives to be shocked by everything. Perhaps we could truly learn from the one who shocks us what is most important even though we may surpass him in external composure and our way of dealing with others. Although good, these latter things are not what is most important; nor is there any reason to desire that everyone follow at once our own path. . . .

The Fourth Dwelling Places

Chapter One

7. Because I have spoken at length on this subject elsewhere, I will say nothing about it here. I only wish to inform you that in order to profit by this path and ascend to the dwelling places we desire, the important thing is not to think much but to love much; and so do that which best stirs you to love. Perhaps we don't know what love is. I wouldn't be very much surprised, because it doesn't consist in great delight but in desiring with strong determination to please God in everything, in striving, insofar as possible, not to offend Him, and in asking Him for the advancement of the honor and glory of His Son and the increase of the Catholic Church. These are the signs of love. Don't think the matter lies in thinking of nothing else, and that if you become a little distracted all is lost.

8. I have been very afflicted at times in the midst of this turmoil of mind. A little more than four years ago I came to understand through experience that the mind (or imagination, to put it more clearly) is not the intellect. I asked a learned man and he told me that this was so; which brought me no small consolation. For since the intellect is one of the soul's faculties, it was an arduous thing for me that it should be so restless at times. Ordinarily the mind flies about quickly, for only God can hold it fast in such a way as to make it seem that we are somehow loosed from this body. I have seen, I think, that the faculties of my soul were occupied and recollected in God while my mind on the other hand was distracted. This distraction puzzled me.

9. O Lord, take into account the many things we suffer on this path for lack of knowledge! The trouble is that since we do not think there is anything to know other than that we must think of You, we do not even know how to ask those who know nor do we understand what there is to ask. Terrible trials are suffered because we don't understand ourselves, and that which isn't bad at all but good we think is a serious fault. This lack of knowledge causes the afflictions of many people who engage in prayer: complaints about interior trials, at least to a great extent, by people who have no learning; melancholy and loss of health; and even the complete abandonment of prayer. For such persons don't reflect that there is an interior world here within us. Just as we cannot stop the movement of the heavens, but they proceed in rapid motion, so neither can we stop our mind; and then the faculties of the soul go with it, and we think we are lost and have wasted the time spent before God. But the soul is perhaps completely joined with Him in the dwelling places very close to the center while the mind is on the outskirts of the castle suffering from a thousand wild and poisonous beasts, and meriting by this suffering. As a result we should not be disturbed; nor should we abandon prayer, which is what the devil wants us to do. For the most part all the trials and disturbances come from our not understanding ourselves.

Chapter Three

Continues on the same subject. Tells about another kind of union the soul can reach with God's help and of how important love of neighbor is for this union.

. . . I hold that it is God's desire that a favor so great not be given in vain; if a person doesn't himself benefit, the favor will benefit others. For since the soul is left with these desires and virtues that were mentioned, it always brings profit to other souls during the time that it continues to live virtuously; and they catch fire from its fire. And even when the soul has itself lost this fire, the inclination to benefit others will remain, and the soul delights in explaining the favors God grants to whoever loves and serves Him.

3. It seems to me that despite all I've said about this dwelling place, the matter is still somewhat obscure. Since so much gain

comes from entering this place, it will be good to avoid giving the impression that those to whom the Lord doesn't give things that are so supernatural are left without hope. True union can very well be reached, with God's help, if we make the effort to obtain it by keeping our wills fixed only on that which is God's will. Oh, how many of us there are who will say we do this, and it will seem to us that we don't want anything else and that we would die for this truth, as I believe I have said! Well I tell you, and I will often repeat it, that if what you say is true you will have obtained this favor from the Lord, and you needn't care at all about the other delightful union that was mentioned. That which is most valuable in the delightful union is what proceeds from this union of which I'm now speaking; and one cannot arrive at the delightful union if the union coming from being resigned to God's will is not very certain. Oh, how desirable is this union with God's will! Happy the soul that has reached it. Such a soul will live tranquilly in this life, and in the next as well. Nothing in earthly events afflicts it unless it finds itself in some danger of losing God or sees that He is offended: neither sickness, nor poverty, nor death—unless the death is of someone who will be missed by God's Church—for this soul sees well that the Lord knows what He is doing better than it knows what it is desiring.

4. You must note that there are different kinds of sufferings. Some sufferings are produced suddenly by our human nature, and the same goes for consolations, and even by the charity of compassion for one's neighbor, as our Lord experienced when He raised Lazarus. Being united with God's will doesn't take these experiences away, nor do they disturb the soul with a restless, disquieting passion that lasts a long while. These sufferings pass quickly. As I have said concerning consolations in prayer, it seems they do not reach the soul's depth but only the senses and faculties. They are found in the previous dwelling places; but they do not enter the last ones still to be explained, since the suspension of the faculties is necessary in order to reach these, as has been said. The Lord has the power to enrich souls through many paths and bring them to these dwelling places, without using the short cut that was mentioned.

5. Nonetheless, take careful note, daughters, that it is necessary for the silkworm to die, and, moreover, at a cost to your-

selves. In the delightful union, the experience of seeing oneself in so new a life greatly helps one to die; in the other union it's necessary that, while living in this life, we ourselves put the silkworm to death. I confess this latter death will require a great deal of effort, or more than that; but it has its value. Thus if you come out victorious the reward will be much greater. But there is no reason to doubt the possibility of this death any more than that of true union with the will of God. This union with God's will is the union I have desired all my life; it is the union I ask the Lord for always and the one that is clearest and safest.

6. But alas for us, how few there must be who reach it, although whoever guards himself against offending the Lord and has entered religious life thinks he has done everything! Oh, but there remain some worms, unrecognized until, like those in the story of Jonah that gnawed away the ivy, they have gnawed away the virtues. This happens through self-love, self-esteem, judging one's neighbors, even though in little things, a lack of charity for them, and not loving them as ourselves. For even though, while crawling along, we fulfill our obligation and no sin is committed, we don't advance very far in what is required for complete union with the will of God.

7. What do you think His will is? . . . the Lord asks of us only two things: love of His Majesty and love of our neighbor. These are what we must work for. By keeping them with perfection, we do His will and so will be united with Him. But how far, as I have said, we are from doing these two things for so great a God as we ought! May it please His Majesty to give us His grace so that we might merit, if we want, to reach this state that lies within our power.

8. The most important sign, in my opinion, as to whether or not we are observing these two laws is whether we observe well the love of neighbor. We cannot know whether or not we love God, although there are strong indications for recognizing that we do love Him; but we can know whether we love our neighbor. And be certain that the more advanced you see you are in love for your neighbor the more advanced you will be in the love of God, for the love His Majesty has for us is so great that to repay us for our love of neighbor He will in a thousand ways increase the love we have for Him. I cannot doubt this.

9. It's important for us to walk with careful attention to how we are proceeding in this matter, for if we practice love of neighbor with great perfection, we will have done everything. I believe that, since our nature is bad, we will not reach perfection in the love of neighbor if that love doesn't rise from love of God as its root. Since this is so important to us Sisters, let's try to understand ourselves even in little things, and pay no attention to any big plans that sometimes suddenly come to us during prayer in which it seems we will do wonders for our neighbor and even for just one soul so that it may be saved. If afterward our deeds are not in conformity with those plans, there will be no reason to believe that we will accomplish the plans. I say the same about humility and all the virtues. Great are the wiles of the devil; to make us think we have one virtue—when we don't—he would circle hell a thousand times. And he is right because such a notion is very harmful, for these feigned virtues never come without some vainglory since they rise from that source, just as virtues from God are free of it as well as of pride.

10. I am amused sometimes to see certain souls who think when they are at prayer that they would like to be humiliated and publicly insulted for God, and afterward they would hide a tiny fault if they could; or, if they have not committed one and yet are charged with it—God deliver us! Well, let anyone who can't bear such a thing be careful not to pay attention to what he has by himself determined—in his opinion—to do. As a matter of fact, the determination was not in the will—for when there is a true determination of the will it's another matter—but a work of the imagination; it is in the imagination that the devil produces his wiles and deceits. And with women or unlearned people he can produce a great number, for we don't know how the faculties differ from one another and from the imagination, nor do we know about a thousand other things there are in regard to interior matters. O Sisters, how clearly one sees the degree to which love of neighbor is present in some of you, and how clearly one sees the deficiency in those who lack such perfection! If you were to understand how important this virtue is for us you wouldn't engage in any other study.

11. When I see souls very earnest in trying to understand the prayer they have and very sullen when they are in it—for it seems

they don't dare let their minds move or stir lest a bit of their spiritual delight and devotion be lost—it makes me realize how little they understand of the way by which union is attained; they think the whole matter lies in these things. No, Sisters, absolutely not; works are what the Lord wants! He desires that if you see a Sister who is sick to whom you can bring some relief, you have compassion on her and not worry about losing this devotion; and that if she is suffering pain, you also feel it; and that, if necessary, you fast so that she might eat—not so much for her sake as because you know it is your Lord's desire. This is true union with His will; and if you see a person praised, the Lord wants you to be much happier than if you yourself were being praised. This, indeed, is easy, for if you have humility you will feel sorry to see yourself praised. But this happiness that comes when the virtues of the Sisters are known is a very good thing; and when we see some fault in them, it is also a very good thing to be sorry and hide the fault as though it were our own.

12. I have said a lot on this subject elsewhere, because I see, Sisters, that if we fail in love of neighbor we are lost. May it please the Lord that this will never be so; for if you do not fail, I tell you that you shall receive from His Majesty the union that was mentioned. When you see yourselves lacking in this love, even though you have devotion and gratifying experiences that make you think you have reached this stage, and you experience some little suspension in the prayer of quiet (for to some it then appears that everything has been accomplished), believe me, you have not reached union. And beg our Lord to give you this perfect love of neighbor. Let His Majesty have a free hand, for He will give you more than you know how to desire because you are striving and making every effort to do what you can about this love. And force your will to do the will of your Sisters in everything, even though you may lose your rights; forget your own good for their sakes no matter how much resistance your nature puts up; and, when the occasion arises, strive to accept work yourself so as to relieve your neighbor of it. Don't think that it won't cost you anything or that you will find everything done for you. Look at what our Spouse's love for us cost Him; in order to free us from death, He died that most painful death on the cross.

Jane Frances de Chantal (1572-1641)

Jeanne de Frémyot was born in Dijon, France on January 23, 1572, daughter of a noble family. Her father was a Catholic statesman and patriot who became president of Burgundy and who arranged her marriage at twenty to the Baron de Chantal, seven years her senior. The marriage was a happy marriage in every respect, and she was able to continue her already devout prayer life throughout. It was not without sadness, however. Only four of their seven children lived to maturity. A greater tragedy befell the Baroness de Chantal when, in 1600, the Baron was accidentally shot by a friend while out hunting. He died nine days later. She remained with her husband's family, devoting her life to her children and to the poor.

In 1604 her father suggested she return to Dijon for Lent; he had arranged for her to hear the preaching of the bishop of Geneva, Frances de Sales. This was the beginning of one of the famous spiritual friendships of history. Jane convinced the bishop, who was five years her senior, to become her spiritual director and advisor. Each believed deeply that their friendship was the work of God.

She apparently wished to enter a Carmelite convent, but he steered her more toward the cooperation with grace as it unfolded within her own circumstances and within the confines of what she could do. He also successfully sought to dispel the scruples with which she had been plagued throughout her life, advising her to "Do all this little by little, gently, as the angels do." In fact, it was three years before he would agree to Jane's desire to enter the religious life.

Sometime later he presented the work he saw for her: an Order devoted to visiting the sick and the poor. This was a striking departure from the Church's understanding of the work of women religious, for at this time vowed women were required to be enclosed. The active works they would take up, if they were to take up any work at all, revolved around the education of girls.

After her eldest daughter married, Jane arranged her other affairs so that her responsibilities could be discharged without her direct presence, and in 1610 she and Francis de Sales founded the Order of the Visitation of Mary (Visitandines). Along with Mary Favre, Charlotte de Brechard, and a servant, Anne Coste, Jane received the habit of the new Order from the bishop in a house near Lake Annecy, not far from where he received his own early education. There the Visitation was erected for women, both young and old, including widows, who wished to live a religious life but did not wish to follow the rigors of strict enclosure. Their common life required common prayer, work, silence, obedience, and strict poverty and, after profession, they were to go out to nurse the sick. This work met with resistance until the archbishop of Lyons, Cardinal de Marquemont, finally insisted on enclosure to grant their order ecclesiastical approbation in 1618. Hence the essentially active Order founded to nurse the sick eventually became an enclosed Order for the education of young girls.

The selections below are taken from conferences she gave her followers. The ordinary asceticism of the day, particularly in Carmels, was not part of the original rule in the spirit of Francis de Sales and Jane Frances de Chantal. While her spirituality was unflinching in its look at interior and exterior virtue, she constantly remembered Francis' recommendation to be gentle with herself, a recommendation she passed to her sisters. She wrote in 1616 to a Visitation nun: "No matter what happens, be gentle and patient with yourself."

The two conferences here, on simplicity and on poverty of spirit, are characteristic of her spirituality, which admitted only to a total and humble self-donation of one's entire being to God. In fact, when asked by one of her sisters what her deepest desire was, she replied that it was indeed to see God, but that she withdrew from possessing even that wish: "The desire of seeing God often comes and knocks at the door of my heart; but I have not opened to it, for I have stripped myself of everything—at least, I wish to do so."

Jane died at Moulins December 13, 1641, and is buried at Annecy near Francis de Sales. She was canonized in 1767, and her feast is celebrated by the universal Church on December 12 and in the United States on August 18.

From Conference XXVIII

On simplicity, poverty of spirit, meekness of heart, and of acquired solid virtue

You have read in a book, you say, that we must have simplicity of life, poverty of spirit, and meekness of heart? My dear Daughter, I am not learned, and therefore I scarcely know how to answer your question. So I shall only say that, in my opinion, simplicity of life is to be simple in our clothing, in our rooms, in our furniture, in our eating, in our conversation, and in all our behavior and actions. And persons are said to be simple in their clothing when they are seen to be plainly dressed, in plain stuff, or at least without fashion; in like manner when anyone has only plain furniture in his dwelling, bed, and everything else, he is said to be simple in bed and household arrangements. When he eats only plain and common food, he is said to be simple in his eating. Likewise, when he is straightforward, frank, artless, and truthful in conversation, he is said to be simple. To have simplicity of life, we must then be simple in all things, also in our affections, wishes, intentions, and aims. Here is the true simplicity, which is highly desirable, and which we must above all things profess; for, we practise it in this that we are treated plainly, and have plain beds and clothing.

Now, for poverty of spirit, this is a detachment from all created things, if we possess them. This poverty of spirit requires us not to set our affections on these, so that we must be poor in these things in affection and will, by having our heart detached and wholly free, being equally contented to have them not or to have them.

Another kind of poverty is to leave them for the love of God, and in order to serve Him more perfectly; not only must we leave them in fact, but also in affection. Indeed, true and perfect poverty of spirit, my dear Daughters, is to have nothing but God in our mind. Oh! how immensely rich this poverty of spirit makes us! because having thus left all things and all which is not God, we come to possess the riches of heaven and of earth, which is God. Let us, then, be poor indeed with this same poverty, seeking God only, wishing God only, attaching ourselves to God only, and we shall be happy in truth, and we shall possess great peace and freedom of spirit.

Meekness of heart, my dear Daughter, means having a heart which is angered by nothing, and offended by nothing that is done to it, which bears with everything, which endures everything, which is compassionate and full of love for our neighbor, which has no bitterness of heart. No, I am not speaking of the heart of flesh: but of the heart of the will and higher part of our soul. Accordingly, the contradictions, persecutions, misfortunes, and difficulties which may happen to the heart that is truly meek, lose their sharpness as soon as they come near it. There are some, in truth, who are naturally meek: so that they already have the business nearly done, and they are greatly beholden to our Lord, who has given them this natural disposition; nevertheless, unless they render it supernatural, it is a very small matter, and they will have no solid virtue. Others, who have not a meek nature, will still be able to acquire this virtue of meekness of heart by God's grace.

Our Blessed Father says that there are two kinds of ways by which God gives us virtues. The first, is by infused grace: for our Lord, Who holds all virtues in His hands, gives them to whom He pleases, and renders souls perfect in an instant, as it happened with St. Paul, with St. Magdalene, with St. Catherine of Genoa, and others who were perfected in an instant; but these are extraordinary graces which we are not to desire, nor expect. The other way of acquiring virtues is ordinary. By the first, God leads to virtue few souls. They are rare, in fact, whom He makes perfect all at once; that depends on His bounty, on His love, which makes Him prevent with His blessings some particular creatures. We are not to promise ourselves, nor presume on deserving this happiness. But our Lord has placed the common way within our attainment, for it is by faithfully corresponding to grace that we shall be able to reach it; and God wills to give the other virtues in this way, since all these Saints have acquired them, as it were, at the sword's point.

You ask now what is solid virtue? My dear Daughter, it is doing all our actions purely for God, practising the virtues as our Lord practised them; for, in all His sufferings and labors on earth, He sought only the pure glory of His Eternal Father, the salvation of creatures, and by no means His own interest and satisfaction. In all that we do, let God's honor, His greater glory, and His good pleasure, be our single aim. In fine, solid virtue is strong, constant, and persevering; for it is not enough to be humble today, but we must be so again tomorrow, and to the very end of our life.

You say: will the soul which has solid virtue (humility, for example) never have a feeling of the humiliations it meets with?

If the soul is well established in this virtue, it will not often have such feeling; nevertheless, it may sometimes happen; but it throws itself at once on God, and annihilates itself so profoundly in His presence and in its own nothingness, that the feeling is dissipated. Our Blessed Father said that he was insensible to the contempt, injuries, and censure with which his actions were treated. Oh! it is in this that we make true acts of humility, when we bear meekly to be humbled, vilified, held for incapable, useless, have no account made of us, all that we do blamed and criticized, submitting ourselves to obedience, seeking contempt, esteeming ourselves the least of all. If it is said in our Rules that the Superior shall keep herself under the feet of all; much more should the Sisters keep themselves at the feet of one another. Oh! my dear Daughters, greatly indeed must we beware of the inclination to esteem ourselves and to have high thoughts, that we may stifle them and go deep into ourselves in good earnest. When there come to us during prayer thoughts and dispositions of humility, how are you to apply them practically, you ask? By practising compliance, obedience; for, my dear Daughter, the greatest acts of humility consist in submission; this is the touchstone for know-

ing whether the holiness and humility which we find in souls are
true. Do you not see that this was the sure mark which the ancient Fathers of the desert had for knowing that St. Simon Stylites
was driven by the Spirit of God, to lead a life so extraordinary
and unusual? Solid virtue, then, is attached to God only, and consists in wishing God only, in depending on God only, in serving
Him equally, constantly, and perseveringly, in whatsoever state
He may put us, whether we be in prosperity or adversity, in joy
or sadness, in consolation or affliction, in health or sickness, in
dryness or delights.

From Conference XXIX

On Perfect Simplicity

Perfect simplicity, my Daughters, consists in having but one
single and sole pretension in all our actions, and that is of pleasing God in all things. The second practice of this virtue which
follows upon the former, is to see only the will of this great God
in all things, good or ill, which befall us; by this means, loving
only that adorable will, our soul will be always tranquil in every
event, even in the delay of our perfection, while we cease not to
labor thereat faithfully. The third practice of simplicity consists
in laying open our faults sincerely, without veiling them. The
fourth is to be truthful in our words, not multiplying them, especially when there is question of justifying ourselves. The fifth,
is to live from day to day, without forethought or care for ourselves, but do well at each moment what is ordered for us, according to our vocation, trusting and committing ourselves to
Divine Providence. If we faithfully employ the present occasions,
we may be certain that greater will be provided for us in working in His Divine service, for our perfection and His glory. We
cannot be truly simple and have so many cares for the future.
Real simplicity prevents reflections on our actions and makes us
artless: if the actions are good, you have no need to consider them;
if they are imperfect, your heart will surely tell you; and, if you
open yourselves to those who direct you, they will be well able
to make this distinction.

I consider that it is an act of great perfection, to conform ourselves in all things to the community, and never to depart from

it by our choice, inasmuch as it is an excellent means to hide from ourselves our perfection. There is found, in this practice, even a certain simplicity of heart so perfect, that it contains all perfection. This sacred simplicity causes the soul to look only to God in all that we do, and to keep itself wholly enclosed in itself in order to give itself to the sole fidelity of the love of its supreme good, by the observance of the Rule, without pouring out its desires in seeking means to do more than that. It will not do out of the way things, which might gain for it the esteem of creatures; but it keeps itself annihilated in itself. It has no great satisfactions, because it does nothing that pleases the will, and nothing more than the community. It seems to itself to be doing nothing; and, in this way, its holiness is hidden from its eyes and its knowledge. God sees it alone, and He takes pleasure in this divine simplicity by which it ravishes His heart, by uniting itself to Him by a wholly pure, wholly simple, and wholly faithful love. It is no longer attentive to follow the lights of its self-love; it no longer listens to its persuasions and will no more look at its own inventions, which would seek self-esteem by great undertakings and by preeminent actions which may make us distinguished from the common.

Such a soul enjoys peace ever tranquil; it can say that it is free to rise above itself, by the possession of the Divine union. Therefore, my Daughters, never think that you are doing very little when you are only following the common path.

Another Fragment on the Same Subject

My dear Sisters, it is true, indeed, that God draws, although in different ways, all the Daughters of the Visitation to Himself, by a certain holy simplicity. Now, this drawing is good when it teaches the soul to depend only on God, to love God only, to obey God only, and in the things of God, and not our own inclinations. I say, and I shall always say, that when God favors a soul with this sacred simplicity and familiarity with Himself; when we see that that renders it more humble and observant, we ought never to turn it aside from it, and it ought never to turn itself aside, however good other ways may seem; for, what more desirable and better good is there than to repose wholly on God? I say that this is the true way and the true holiness of that soul;

if it turns away from this, it puts itself in danger of resisting God, and making Him withdraw from it; and, afterwards, it will have a great deal of trouble to return to its place; I know not even if it will return.

I know not why the heart of man is so foolish; is not God the God of the heart, can He not, then, give the attraction which He knows to be most suitable? Yes, Sisters, our hearts are created for God, and have no repose but in Him. Let us, then, do our all to fix them absolutely in this Divine centre; and, once we find them there, let us never turn them away therefrom, otherwise we should be guilty before God.

God is the treasure of the pure and faithful soul; when then it has its treasure, let it enjoy it without desiring other things. The perfection of the Daughters of the Visitation is to be founded on four stones, otherwise their edifice will fall: profound humility, candid simplicity, sweet meekness and condescension, and the complete abandonment of themselves into the arms of Divine Providence and of their Superior. This is the effectual means of arriving at the perfection of our holy calling.

Mary Ward (1585–1645)

Mary Ward was born Catholic in York, England, during a time when her inherited faith was severely persecuted. No less were the persecutions she suffered at the hands of her own, however, as she sought to form a new way for women to actively serve the Church in the manner of the Society of Jesus, as women contemplatives in action. The concept was anathema to a seventeenth-century Church that sought to have women remain enclosed. Mary Ward and her followers in the Institute of the Blessed Virgin Mary, as it came to be known, were derided as "jesuitesses," yet they were the first international experiment of active women religious, vowed to poverty, chastity, and obedience, and who would model their rule and spirituality on that of St. Ignatius.

Her own writings show her filled with Ignatian spirituality, graced with the ability to see God in all things, and willing to suffer greatly for the sake of following God's will. The lesson she has left is that it is the ability and the willingness to distinguish God's will from that of others, including oneself, that makes all the difference and indeed creates both the need and ability for additional self sacrifice.

Mary's life was, in many respects, a long loneliness spent waiting for the Lord's will to be recognized in the founding, and then refounding, of her Institute after its suppression. In early seventeenth-century England it was too dangerous for the few remaining scattered nuns to accept novices so, in 1606, friends gave her an introduction to the English Jesuits in Belgium who quickly placed her in a Belgian Poor Clare novitiate. As it turned out, her vocation was not nurtured, but deflected, by both the Jesuits and the

Poor Clares. She left in 1607 and founded an English Poor Clare convent which she sought to place in the charge of the Jesuits. Since Jesuits are forbidden by their rule to have charge of convents, she eventually worked out the practical solution of having Jesuits as spiritual directors. But she soon left her fledgling convent, feeling that her call was beyond the cloister.

By 1609 she returned to St. Omer with five "English Ladies" who lived in community and taught young children. As their numbers grew, so did their difficulties, for the major rules for women, those of Augustine, Benedict, Francis, and Teresa, each demanded cloister, as did the newer foundations, the Ursulines (1535) and the Visitation nuns (1610), which had bowed to ecclesiastical pressure for enclosure. She adapted the Jesuit *Formula Instituti* and walked from Brussels to Rome to present it to Pope Gregory XV in 1621. As she futilely awaited the rule's approval her houses multiplied, and so did her troubles. The Institute was suppressed by Urban VII in 1631, its property was confiscated, and Mary was jailed by the Inquisition as a heretic. There were three hundred nuns in the Institute at the time, and, except in England and in Munich, all their houses were closed. Some few members clung together, permitted only private vows. The Institute remained alive and grew, after a great while with papal approval. In 1909, three hundred years after its founding, the Institute, as well as the Sisters of Loretto, was allowed to call Mary Ward its founder. In 1978, with Jesuit approval, the Institute took the constitutions of the Society of Jesus.

Mary Ward saw the Lord's hand in everything, even in adversity, and never failed to trust that His will would be done in her. She died in 1645 and was buried in a Protestant churchyard at Osbaldwick, England, where a marker reads: "To love the poor, persevere in the same, live die and rise with them was all the aim of Mary Ward who, having lived 60 years and 8 days died the 30th of Jan. 1645."

The original manuscripts of the selections here are in the Institute Archives in Munich (AIM), and transcriptions provided by the Institute were modernized with its approval. The first is a retrospective look at her vocation written in 1620, in which she says she could not leave for Europe until she was twenty-one. The second and third selections describe the long loneliness as she waits to undertake God's will with the approval of the Church. In the final selection she speaks of death and of her understanding that she is unimportant except insofar as she is an instrument of God's will.

Letter to the Apostolic Nuncio of Lower Germany, Monsignor Albergato, 1620

. . . . At 15 I found myself called to religion, after which time I could take no content in any worldly estate. Hindered by parents, and other worldly encumbrances, I could not get into these parts, till the age 21. I had no particular vocation to one order more than another, only it seemed to me most perfect to take the most austere that so a soul might give herself to God, not in part, but altogether, since I saw not how a religious woman could do good to more than herself alone. To teach children seemed then too much distraction [and] might be done by others, nor was [it] of that perfection and importance as therefore to hinder that quiet and continual communication with God which strict enclosure afforded. Enclosure, and the perfect observance of poverty, were the two special points I aimed at in whatsoever order I should enter, being (as I said) I could do no good to others, which if it could have been, I valued above all, though I found a far more sensible contentment in solitude and abstraction from the world, and therefore never so much as thought of that other (in way of practice) till God (as I trust) called me unto it in a manner against my will.

What happened in the first 4 years after I came over would be too tedious and troublesome for [you] to read; in which space, a monastery was erected for such of our nation as desired to render themselves Poor Clares, in which holy order I intended to live and die, for the reasons aforesaid. The business of the monastery ended, but the space not yet habitable, the religious that were brought out of another monastery to begin that were placed in a secular house [near] by, and we that were to enter with them, who altogether observed the rule of Saint Clare in full perfection, in which practice I found singular content, and now began to feel a great tranquility of mind, often comforted to think that after an 11 year withholding and turbation, the rest of my days should be spent in quiet and with God alone.

This quiet lasted many weeks, [until] . . . came suddenly upon me such an alteration and disposition as the operation of an inexpressible power could only cause, with a sight and certainty that there I was not to remain, that some other thing was to be done by me, but what in particular was not shown. The change and alteration this wrought for half an hour or more was extraordinary. I saw not anything, but understood more clearly that this was to be so than if I had seen, or heard it spoken. To leave what I loved so much and enjoyed with such sensible contentment; to expose myself to new labors which then I saw to be very many; to incur the several censures of men and the great oppositions which on all sides would happen (appearing at that time as afterwards I found them) afflicted me exceedingly; yet had I no power to will, or wish any other than to expose myself to all these inconveniences and put myself into God's hands with these uncertainties. By the advice of my confessor I continued the practice of that austere life half a year longer, the better to discover from whence that light came.

When the rest were to be clothed I departed from them (my confessor telling me I might be saved, either going or staying, which was all the encouragement or assistance any alive gave me at that time.) I made a vow of perpetual chastity and another to obey my confessor in this particular [matter], that if, or when, he should command me to enter into the Teresians I would obey. This they counseled me unto, and though I found no particular vocation to that order, yet hoping God would not leave me nor forbear to dispose me to his best will, for leaving myself for him, I did as they advised me, which caused me great trouble afterward [in] many ways, though all turned to my best in the end. I made a third vow to spend some months in England to do all the little I could for God and the good of those there, not to be idle in the meantime, and the better prepared for whatsoever God should call me to.

Being there, and thus employed, I had a second infused light in manner as before, but much more distinct: that the work to be done was not a monastery of Teresians, but a thing much more grateful to God and so great an augmentation of his glory as I cannot declare, but not any particulars what, how, and in what manner such a work should be; which after this light was past I reflected upon with some sadness, for though in that instant of time my understanding was clearly convinced that the thing then put before me was truly good and the same which reason itself would have effected, and my will so possessed as left without power then or ever after to love or elect any contrary thing. Yet to have still all denied me, and nothing proposed in particular seemed somewhat hard, and besides I was anxious how to govern my affection for the present in these two contraries, as not to have a contrary will to what I had vowed (which was to enter into the Teresians when I should be commanded), neither to be unanswerable to that which then seemed to be God Almighty's determination (which was not to be Teresian but some other thing.) God help me in this, as I trust he will in all.

My purpose of time of stay in England expired, I returned to Saint Omers. Diverse [women] followed with intention to be religious where I should be, living together there. Great insistance was made by diverse spiritual and learned men that we would take upon us some rule already confirmed. Several rules were procured by our friends, both from Italy and France, and we earnestly urged to make choice of some of them. They seemed not that which God would have done and the refusal of them caused much persecution, and the more, because I denied all, and could not say what in particular I desired or found myself called unto.

About this time in the year 1611 I fell sick in great extremity; being somewhat recovered (by a vow made to send in pilgrimage to our Blessed Lady of Sichem), being alone, in some extraordinary repose of mind, I heard distinctly, not by sound of voice but intellectually understood, these words: Take the same of the Society, so understood as that we were to take the same both in matter and manner, that only excepted which God by diversity of sex hath prohibited. These few words gave so great measure of light in that particular Institute, comfort and strength, and changed so the whole soul, as that impossible for me to doubt but that they came from him, whose words are works. My confessor resisted, all the Society opposed; diverse institutes were drawn by several persons, some of which were approved, and greatly commended by the last Bishop Blasius of Saint Omers, our so great friend, and some other divines. These were offered us and as it were pressed upon us; there was no remedy but refuse them, which caused infinite troubles. These would they needs that at least we should take the name of some order confirmed, or some new one, or any we could think of, so not that of Jesus. This the Fathers of the Society urged exceedingly (and do still every day), telling us that to any such name we may take what constitutions we will, even theirs in substance, if otherwise we will not be satisfied; but by no means will they that we observe that form which their constitutions and rules are written in, which, say they, are not essential or needful. The neglect of these offers did and do cause extreme troubles, especially for the first 7 years, while my confessor (whom I had tied myself to obey) lived; they urging him in many things to say as they said, though against his own judgement and knowledge, as after I understood, neither could he yield unto them in all. One time in particular they urged him so much about the name, as that he made answer to diverse grave Fathers, that if their case were his they durst not urge any change.

Concerning the name I have twice in several years understood, in as particular a manner as these other things I have recounted, that the denomination of these must be Jesus. And thrice, I think more often, of the inconveniences would happen to both parties, if ours should have any dependency of the Fathers of the Society. The several great effects of those former words were too many to recount. The continual light God gives in little and great, appertaining to the true practice of this Institute, is such as cannot easily be declared. And the progress of so many souls as are now of this Company if you know the particulars of their proceedings so as some other less interested might recount them together with the miraculous calls of several of them, it would manifestly appear that God's hand were in the work, and that His Majesty is well pleased with the manner hitherto observed, which is no other than what in this other paper I humbly here present.

Letter to Win Campian, Vice-Superior at Naples

I think, dear child, the trouble and the long loneliness you heard me speak of is not far from [me], which whensoever it is, happy success will follow; you are the first I have uttered this conceit so plainly to, pray for me and the work. It grieves me I cannot have you also with me to help to bear a part, but a part you will bear howsoever.

AIM Various Papers, No. 10

"The Loneliness"

How severely God punishes sin except we do penance

I saw it pleased God better that I should satisfy in this life; and to content him I besought him earnestly to show me wherein or by what way he would have me make satisfaction (for he was near me). I considered that to forbear sin I had already resolved and was bound, except I would incur more need of satisfaction. There occurred that I should bear *well* all such difficulties as might happen in the doing of his will.

I thought this was little, and that no great difficulty could happen, considering my disposition of mind and freedom. I therefore begged more earnestly to know the thing that he would have done, promising that whatsoever it were I would do it.

The same was before me still, and nothing else. After some time I thought that that might be the same, that God would have me satisfy by, and that perhaps I might find more difficulties and crosses in the passages of my life than I did imagine. I then offered myself to suffer with love and gladness whatsoever trouble or contrariety should happen in my doing of his will, but besought him withall that none of those things might hinder what his will was to have done. Presented [with the possibility] that perchance there was some great trouble to happen about the confirmation of our course, with this I found a great and new love for this Institute and a near embracing or union of affection with it. I offered myself willingly to this difficulty and besought our Lord with tears that he would give me grace to bear it, and that no contradiction might hinder his will (whatever his will, *for I had then a greater love to his will in general than to any particular*).

I was as though the occasion had been present. I saw there was
no help nor comfort for me, but to cleave fast to him, and so
I did, for he was there to help me. I besought him that the love
I felt to this course now might support me then, when the trouble
should happen, because perhaps I should not then have means
or force or time to dispose myself or to call so particularly upon
him. I begged of him with much affection that this prayer I now
made might serve as a petition for his grace at that time. I left
with a solid contentment, and, as I recall it, desirous to serve and
suffer for God; but I knew such a thing would certainly happen.

AIM Various Papers, No. 15, 1618

"Of Death"

Sadness and darkness for a good space, neither desiring nor react-
ing [to] anything. Using more diligence to descend to particulars,
I found a loathing to leave this company before its cause was
confirmed—lest those that followed might make it something
else—and here (against my will) I seemed of some importance,
and not be spared without prejudice to the work, this I knew to
be a lie, and to proceed from no good ground. I humbled myself
(though with some difficulty) and confessed the power of God,
to do what he would have done by any [means] (because I per-
ceived this only by faith I was bound to believe so). I begged of
God to be rid of this, and sought to find reasons to make myself
appear in my own sight for such as I was. Somewhat troubled,
I repeated often that he could do what he would and by whom
he would, asking of myself: why not by any other as well as by
me? Looking back how all in the beginning my call to this course
had passed, I saw by particulars (good for me to note at leisure,
but too long to set here) how hardly and with how much ado
I was brought by God to do what little I have done. Something
I found by the sight of those particulars clearly convinced my
judgement that God's working was the beginning, middle, end,
and sole cause why. That with those graces, anyone else would
have been moved as soon, and many far sooner, and that this
good had no being, nor place in me, but by the only working
of his grace, which though in me yet a different thing from *me*,
without which I would need that this good could not stand and
which, withdrawn I should remain as before. Then turning to God

with intent to confess my own nothingness, I found (that by force of will, against knowledge) I would still be of importance and a needful person. Then sad, I said what, still something in my own sight, notwithstanding all these reasons, and truths to be contrary! Well, my Lord, I am contented with this want. Pardon it and punish it as thou please.

Coming to conclude, and offering myself to God, I saw myself little, and of less importance for this work. God's will, and wisdom seemed great, and his power such, and of such force, as strongly to affect in an instant, or with a look, whatsoever he would. And before this greatness, *the power* of all his creatures together (*resisting him*) melted away, and in a moment, ceased to be. I turned to myself again, offering with love to leave what I loved, very desirous to die before *this* occurred, that his working in it might the more appear. Then, moved not to desire anything but God's will, I inwardly said: neither life, nor death, my God, but thy holy will be ever done in me, do what pleases you the best. Only this, let me no more offend thee; nor fail to do, what thou would have me [do].

The hour seemed, not half of one, I besought him, that this, which I now saw and did, might support me when I lay dying, because perchance those extremes would then make me unfit for all.

This remains [with me] still and I find a great desire to die *before*, so that God's glory and this deceit of my inability may the better appear. But it seems my security, and best [choice is] to rest in God's will only, which I do, and will for ever.

Jeanne Marie Guyon (1648–1717)

Jeanne Marie Bouvier de la Mothe Guyon is one of the most famous of the champions of "quietism," a generally disregarded spiritual movement primarily associated with seventeenth-century Italy and France. The quietism of the Spanish spiritual director in Rome, Miguel de Molinos, was actually condemned as heretical by Pope Innocent XI in 1687. Jeanne Marie Guyon did not escape the controversy. She endured ecclesiastical wrath at the fact that a woman presumed to divulge spiritual principles and give spiritual advice and from the fact that her teachings countered some of the established modes of thinking about spirituality.

She spent most of her childhood in various convents and developed a deep attraction first to romances and then to mystical writings, resulting in a strong and apparently unguided prayer life. Jeanne Marie married Jacques Guyon du Chesnoy, an invalid two dozen years her senior, when she was sixteen. He died when she was twenty-eight, leaving her with two children. A few years later she left her son with relatives and took her daughter with her to Geneva, from whence she struck out to spread her doctrine of "quietism," as she presented it to her director, Barnabite Father François La Combe. Teaching quietism became her mission. She traveled throughout Switzerland, Italy, and France between 1671–1686, often with La Combe. Either they or their enemies aroused a great deal of suspicion about their work: La Combe earned life imprisonment for his efforts, and she spent her remaining years in and out of various convents, predominantly under house arrest, or in prison. One of her most famous disciples was the bishop of Cambrai, François de Salignac de la Mothe Fénelon, who also suffered as a result of the controversy. While she may be an intellectual cousin of de Molinos, she apparently developed her theories independent of those who were spreading quietism on the continent, and to her death she claimed she knew nothing of de Molinos' teachings.

At the time, proponents of a highly methodic and imaginative consideration of the humanity of Jesus through Ignatian meditation were in conflict with those who supported a more contemplative approach, and each of the many proponents of various spiritualites was adopting and adapting the same or similar terms to present conflicting concepts. Among the difficulties in Jeanne Marie Guyon's method was her explanation of the notion of "quiet" in prayer. While apparently not far from Teresa's prayer of quiet in the higher levels of the Interior Castle, it allowed her opponents to raise questions about grace and free will: did the quiet she referred to exist as an example of infused grace, or was it an acquired habit?

In fact, Jeanne Marie Guyon's discussions of prayer center on abandonment, and her discussions of life center on renunciation. The concepts, when not seen in a healthy light, become the sort of quietism of which we are well warned, and can even devolve into an approach of pre-destination. The single wicket through which one must go, in her method, is that of renunciation of the will, an act which presupposes all other acts of renunciation, particularly those within prayer. Continual self-surrender, to the exigencies of life and to the vicissitudes of prayer, makes one "quiet." One must abandon all desire, including the desire for salvation.

Such absolute passivity is dangerous, and her preachings apparently did not contain sufficient warnings to temper their attractive nature. Some commentators suggest she actually did experience the prayer of quiet when young, and she trusted her own experience to the point that she was attacked for lacking the supreme female virtues of her age: humility and docility. Considering how vulnerable she made herself through her belief, perhaps now we ought view her zeal with a new optic.

In any event, there is a great deal to be learned from Jeanne Marie Guyon. She was unquestionably influenced by the thought of the Enlightenment. Her *A Short Method of Prayer*—in which she argues that prayer makes us human—was fashionable among the aristocracy of her day. A prayer of abandonment, she wrote, allows us to depend wholly on God, who acts in our lives through His creatures.

In addition to *A Short Method of Prayer*, from which a small selection appears below, she wrote poems, spiritual canticles, and many letters. Letter 52, translated here, characteristically speaks of the advantages and necessity of abandonment of self to bring one to pure faith and a simple clinging to God alone, and it underscores the necessity of humility and simplicity in order to be at peace with God and with oneself.

Jeanne Marie Guyon lived in a century filled with spiritual conflict and controversy. Where her thought is related to the quietism of her contemporary de Molinos, it is as well related to that of Jean de Caussade many years later. Without supporting one or another of the parties in the quietist controversy, it is possible to gain insight into healthy renunciation through the work of Jeanne Marie Guyon.

From *A Short Method of Prayer*

Chapter 1

Prayer is nothing more than the turning of the heart of God, and the interior exercise of love. St. Paul tells us to pray without ceasing (I Thess. 5:17), the Lord says the same. (Mark 13:33,37) Everyone is capable of prayer, and everyone should do so. . . .

Chapter 5

Here true abandonment and consecration to God should begin, by our deep conviction that everything that happens is the will of God and therefore meant for us.

This conviction will leave us content with everything and will let us see even the simplest events as from the hand of God and not from His creatures.

I beg you, who are desirous of giving yourself to God, not to withdraw yourself once you have turned yourself over to Him, and to remember that your gift, once given, is no longer at your disposal. Abandonment is the key to the inner life; perfection follows complete abandonment.

Hang onto your abandonment, then, without listening to reason or reflection. A great faith makes for great abandonment; you must completely trust God, against hope believing in hope (Rom. 4:18). Abandonment is the letting go of the care of ourselves so that we may be guided entirely by God.

We are all called to abandonment . . . which ought to be an utter leaving of ourselves, both outwardly and inwardly, in the hands of God, forgetting ourselves and thinking only of Him. Thereby the heart is kept free and contented.

Practically speaking, it should be the continual loss of our own will in the will of God, a renunciation of all natural inclinations, however good they may appear, in order to be left free to choose only as God chooses: we should be indifferent to all things, whether temporal or spiritual, whether for the body or for the soul. Forget the past, trust the future, and give the present wholly to God. We should be content with the present moment, which carries with it God's eternal will, and attribute nothing which happens to us to the creature, but see all things in God, and coming infallibly from His hand, excepting only our own sin.

Leave yourself, then, to be guided by God as He will, both in your interior and exterior life.

Letter 52

1. Get out of yourself, my friend. As long as you hang on to your own thoughts and your own will, for every sort of pretext you can imagine, you will never enter into pure prayer or pure love; you will never become holy. Your imagination will never be free

of dreams, your spiritual thoughts will only be unsettled; you will never be free because you will always be wrapped up in yourself, unsettled, looking for what you do not have, bored and disgusted with what you do have: your heart will never be satisfied and you will never reach perfect peace: you will continually carry yourself around and you will find yourself particularly burdened and uncomfortable; you will never enjoy the pure light of truth; your enlightenment will always be clouded by the objections of reason and, consequently, will always be off the mark: you will be an example of a gloomy faith, a faith that will never be released from all things and from all concerns.

2. A pure and plain faith unfailingly allows the soul to overcome the objections of thought and reason and place itself permanently in the serene and peaceful place where truth resides, and from which one can see all the piled up presumptions of humanity. It is true that the simple, pure and detached faith, by which we are united to the simple Essence, makes us enter into it as long as we are not restrained by and put upon by whatever may occur, good or bad. The spirit thus revealed by faith, and the will made plain by love, each enters into this pure and simple love detached of all self-interest, whatever it may be, detached of all falling back or fixing on the self, resting lost in time and eternity without self-concern: staying uniquely attached to this great object, we let it do with us what it will, happy in whatever state we find ourselves, or whatever place it puts us, even happy in our own suffering and poverty, because it remains what it is, a great unchangeable ALL, infinitely happy. My unhappiness does not have the ability to affect its happiness, and I cannot change it at all.

3. Remember well, my dear friend, and do not ever forget, that whatever takes you away from the world and turns you to God is the best state to be in. That which makes us die to our own self-worth is excellent, and to our short-sighted and narrow ways of looking for perfection, is the best because it is to the greater glory of God. You have well understood and practiced the exterior virtues up to now, but you have not well understood the perfect abnegation of self, which has a signal influence: the complete abandonment of your judgement and your will. You have not at all comprehended this simple, small and perfect obedience, as much toward God as toward others, this kind of obedience which comes from true humility, and which does not hang on

to any self-will at all and which is able to judge the nature of submission, nor have you understood He who commands, examines,
and weighs it.

4. There are some people who follow their own reason in place
of submitting to the Eternal Reason. These people always stay
within their own notions of prudence, and never participate in
the wisdom of Jesus Christ, the most humble and obedient individual who ever existed. This is hardly the practice of the virtue
of humility, which comes from complete self-knowledge and
which is a self abnegation produced by renunciation of will, that
is, the humility and obedience which become so well-suited to
the soul that it practices them completely, naturally, and almost
unconsciously.

5. You are very far from this, even though you may seem to have
exterior perfection, you have not yet arrived at this point. But
it is what God wants of you, and something to which he calls
you. You cannot fulfill your vocation without it. My dear child,
that I may turn all your days toward Jesus Christ in his sorrows
and his agonies, I say to you with the Apostle: "Do not become
proud of your own prudence" (Rom 12:16), but abandon yourself totally to Jesus Christ, so that he can lead you not by human
wisdom but by the foolishness of the cross, by your childlike simplicity, by all those things which he calls you, to which privilege
you have not yet responded.

6. I have a great fear that instead of becoming simple and little,
to which you are of course naturally opposed, you will not become wiser and bigger! "If you do not become like a child you
will not enter the kingdom of God;" (Matt 18:3) you will not become possessed by God, you will stay perplexed, floating, doubt-
ful, uncertain, indeterminant, held back by your own sense of
self without taking the right course, that which is the will of God.
"I thank you, Father, for you have hidden your secrets from the
great and wise, and have revealed them to the small: yes, Father,
because you have willed it" (Matt 11:25-26). What I want, my
dear child, is that you follow this advice that I give you on be-
half of God. "Fire and water, the good and the bad, are before
your eyes, it is up to you to choose" (Sir 15:16). If you do not
follow the advice I give you here, I fear you will go off the road
of truth without anyone to help you. There will be many bad

things before you know it; it will become nearly impossible to get back on the right road: I can see it well, I will die of unhappiness. I hope that you will always do as I say here, and that you will become through this my consolation and my joy; Amen, Jesus.

Elizabeth Bayley Seton (1774–1821)

Elizabeth Seton was born in the United States on August 28, 1774, probably in New York, and died at forty-six in Emmitsburg, Maryland, having founded the Sisters of Charity in the United States. The daughter of Dr. Richard Bayley and Catherine Charlton, Elizabeth was raised in the relative wealth of upper-class New York Episcopal society. Her parents had three children before her mother died when Elizabeth was three, and her father remarried, giving Elizabeth six additional siblings. In 1794, at nineteen, she married the wealthy shipping merchant William McGee Seton, and they had five children—Anna Maria, William, Richard, Catherine, and Rebecca—who were left fatherless when he died of tuberculosis in Pisa, Italy in 1803. Elizabeth and her daughter, Anna Maria, were with him when he died.

Her spiritual life is well documented in letters, journals, and "remembrances" written over the course of approximately twenty-five years, and particularly in letters to her friend Julia Scott and to the members of the Filicci family in Leghorn, Italy. After her husband died she remained in Italy for several months, returning to New York in June 1804. With the encouragement of the Filiccis, her understanding of the Catholic doctrine of presence in Eucharist drew her to Catholicism, and she became a Roman Catholic in March 1805. Her letter to Amabilia Filicci, below, recounts her joy at her First Communion.

She moved to Baltimore in 1808 and, at the invitation of the archbishop of Baltimore and of the president of neighboring St. Mary's College, opened an academy for girls. Her journal notes of this period show her ever increasing devotion to the mystery of presence in the Eucharist. Her prayer was constantly complemented by service, and her letter to Rose Stubbs presents the simplest of mission statements: "a religious life devoted to the education of poor children in the catholic faith." Elizabeth made private vows in 1809, and that year she and four companions became the first American Sisters of Charity. They adopted the rule of St. Vincent de Paul in 1812 and they pronounced public vows a year later, following a retreat given by Elizabeth.

Her letters and journals can be difficult for the twentieth century reader, full as they are of the whirls and flourishes of late eighteenth-century writing, and are here edited with modern punctuation. Throughout her work there is the development of a singleminded attachment to Eucharist, and to the children, both her own and those who came to be in her care. She is practical and caring, sympathetic and stern, and invariably respectful of all.

During her lifetime the Sisters of Charity opened several schools and institutions, particularly the first Catholic child-care institution in Philadelphia, in 1814, and another in New York in 1817. Her cause of canonization was begun by the archbishop of Baltimore, James Cardinal Gibbons, in 1903, and she was proclaimed saint by Pope Paul VI on September 14, 1975, the first native-born American so honored.

The selections below are representative of the wide range of her writings. In the first, she recounts her First Communion to Amabilia Filicci; the second is from her personal journal; the third is her invitation to Rose Stubbs to join her congregation; and the last is from her 1813 retreat to her sisters.

Journal, March 25, 1805

At last Amabilia, at last, God is mine and I am His. Now let all go its round. I have received Him. The awful impressions of the evening before, fears of not having done all to prepare, and yet even then transports of confidence and hope in his goodness.

My God! To the last breath of life will I not remember this night of watching for morning dawn, the fearful beating heart so pressing to be gone, the long walk to town? But every step counted nearer that street, then nearer that tabernacle, then nearer the moment he would enter the poor, poor little dwelling so all his own.

And when he did the first thought I remember was: "let God arise, let his enemies be scattered." For it seemed to me my King had come to take his throne and instead of the humble, tender welcome I had expected to give him it was but a triumph of joy and gladness that the deliverer was come and my defence and shield and strength and Salvation [was] made mine for this world and the next.

Now then, all the excesses of my heart found their play and it danced with much more fervor. No, [I] must not say that. But, perhaps almost with as much as the royal Prophets before his Ark, for I was far richer than he and more honored than he ever could be. Now the point is for the fruits. So far, truly, I feel all the powers of my soul held fast by him who came with so much Majesty to take possession of this little poor Kingdom.

. . . he has proved well enough to me there what he is, and I can say, with even more transports than St. Thomas, my Lord and my God. Truly, it is a greater Mystery how Souls shut themselves out by incredulity from his best of all Gifts, this Divine Sacrifice and Holy Eucharist, refusing to believe in spiritual and heavenly order of things that Word which spake and created the Whole Natural Order, recreating through succession of ages for the body, and yet he cannot be believed to recreate for the soul. I see more mystery in this blindness of redeemed souls than in any of the mysteries proposed in his church. With what grateful and unspeakable joy and reverence I adore the daily renewed virtue of that Word by which we possess him in our blessed Mass and Communion. But all that is but Words, since Faith is from God and I must humble myself and adore.

Your [Antonio] goes now for England and will soon be with you, I trust. Much he says of my bringing all the children to your [house at] Gubbio, to find peace and abundance, but I have a long life of Sins to expiate and, since I hope always to find the morning Mass in America, it matters little what can happen through the few successive days I may have to live, for my health is pitiful. Yet we will see. Perhaps our Lord will pity my little ones. At all events, happen now that I will rest with God, the tabernacle and Communion, so now I can pass the Valley of Death itself.

Antonio will tell you all our little affairs.

Pray for your own EAS.

Journal, probably about 1809

There is a Mystery, the greatest of all my stories. Not that my adored Lord is in the Blessed Sacrament of the Altar. His word has said it, and what is so simple as to take that word, which is the Truth itself? But that Souls of his own creation, whom he gave his Life to save, Who are endowed with his choicest gifts in all things else, should remain blind, insensible, and deprived of that light without which every other blessing is unavailing! — and that the ungrateful, stupid, faithless being to whom *He* has given the Free and Bounteous Heavenly gift shall approach his true and Holy Sanctuary, taste the sweetness of his presence, feed on the bread of Angels, the Lord of glory united to the very essence of its Being and become a part of itself, yet still remain a groveler in the Earth! It (my poor, poor Soul) is what we too well experience while lost in wonder of his forebearing Mercy, and still more wondering at our own misery in the very center of Blessedness. Jesus, then, *is there*. We can go, receive him, *he is our own*. Were we to pause and think of this thro' Eternity, yet we can only realize it by his conviction: that *he is there* (O heavenly theme!) is as certainly true as that Bread naturally taken removes my hunger. So this Bread of Angels removes my pain, my cares, warms, cheers, soothes, contents and renews my whole being. Merciful God, and I do possess you, kindest, dearest Friend, every affection of my Nature absorbed in you still is Active, nay, perfected in their operations thro' your refining love.

February 20, 1809

My dear dear Rose,

. . . A gentleman here who is about to take the tonsure has given a handsome property for the establishment of such females who may choose to lead a religious life devoted to the education of poor children in the catholic faith, and I am already the Mother of some & have the prospect of receiving many daughters. We are going to begin our Novitiate in a beautiful country place in the mountains, and if ever by the providence of God you feel an inclination to join us, and your dear parents would think proper to consent, there will be a happy home ready for you which you may enter without expense or difficulty, but so great a happiness as that of receiving my dear Rose in my arms is more than I dare expect.

Notes from the community retreat Elizabeth Seton gave in July, 1813, prior to their pronouncing vows on July 19, the feast of St. Vincent de Paul

God alone can be thy *all*, his heaven thy worthy mansions, his eternity the only sufficient time of enjoyments with thee. Dost thou see that his infinite love wants thee? Thou art betrothed to him for a spouse, and he waits for thee, or, rather, cannot wait, and comes to visit the lower dwellings. He comes in Bethlehem, a dearest & most amiable child, to obtain thy tenderest love & play before thee in his cradle. Thy God—infant in swaddling clothes—he lives a long while in the land of thy exile to teach thee the ways of his heavens. And how thou must please him like an amiable spouse. He sees that his enemy and thine has covered thee with wounds and quite disfigured thee all over and lo! It is in his very blood he would have thee redeemed, revived, restored to utmost purity & beauty. . .all his love is given up for thee with inexpressible love. It *was* his passion and death; it *is* daily and hourly in graces of every kind. O Spouse of such love, will thou not care to please him exceedingly? Wilt thou not be more sensible of thy happy end and glorious excellence?

Peace to the Daughters of Charity in the Spirit of faith, as having only one heavenly Father, one only same savior Jesus, one only same Spouse and Sanctifier of all—the Holy Ghost . . . peace, the most sincere, truly from the secret heart and full heart as in the presence of their dear Lord, who searches incessantly the heart itself. Peace in mutual honor and esteem, respecting, as says St. Paul, all others better than ourselves. None of all so great a sinner, so frail an abuser of grace as we are. Peace in the perfect union of intentions, consecration, search of divine love and heavenly things, desires of every good thing for our soul and the souls of others, which reigns here among us all. Peace for the promoting of this precious family of St. Joseph, knowing how much its future welfare depends on the graces we shall *now* bring on it, those graces which the smiles of our Lord will grant but in proportion as he shall see the blessings of peace improve among us. Peace also in a courageous spirit of mortification and penance, knowing how much dearer to our Lord are the victims of peace offered to him than the poor, angry, selfish hearts which we bring every morning and many times a day at the foot of his altar. Peace at the sight of that heavenly tabernacle where still abides so silently & peaceably, in such striking self-annihilation this, our divine *Jesus*, who said only of himself that he was meek and humble of heart. O peace to our miserable self love, the general cause of all our trials, nine times of ten the miserable occasion of our faults. Sweet Lord, pity now the sorrows of the daughters of thy kinder charity. Bid their hearts truly enjoy thy peace among them all, and leave here to their successors the most abundant grace and goodly example of peace.

Edith Stein (1891–1942)

Edith Stein was born to Jewish parents on Yom Kippur, October 12, 1891, and died a Carmelite nun at Auschwitz on August 9, 1942.

The youngest of eleven children, she early on exhibited an introspective acceptance of reality that would mark all her writing. By her own account, she did not repudiate God at the age of fifteen, she simply forgot about him. This forgetfulness lasted until she was twenty-four, just one year before the completion of her doctoral studies under the phenomenologist Edmund Husserl, when she began to recognize an interior call to a relationship with God. She was awarded the doctorate in 1917 with a dissertation *On the Problem of Empathy*, which was met by both scholarly objection and praise. She was unable to find a teaching position, and so worked as a research assistant to Husserl for a time until, frustrated by his inattention to detail and unwillingness to work at coalescing his thought, she quit.

For some time after leaving Husserl she earned a living as a lecturer, gaining an international reputation in Germany, Switzerland, and Austria. In late 1921 she by happenstance picked a copy of Teresa of Avila's *The Book of Her Life* from a bookshelf while visiting with friends. The varied strands of her thought suddenly converged into an immediate desire to be baptized a Catholic, and so she was on January 1, 1922, shortly thereafter being confirmed. She saw her instruction and conversion as preparation for entry to Carmel, but her mother had suffered so much as the result of her conversion that she decided to delay her entrance. So she took a job teaching with the Dominican sisters at Speyer, and lived with them in community as an oblate for eight years. During this time she wrote numerous letters of spiritual direction to women which, for the most part, have neither been published nor translated to English.

After leaving Speyer she applied for a teaching position at Freiburg, and was cordially welcomed there by Martin Honecker and Martin Heidegger. But no job materialized then or later as she continued to lecture across German-speaking Europe. In 1933 she briefly held a position at the Catholic Pedagological Institute of Münster, a position that evaporated in the light of Nazism. Here she saw providence, for her only other employment possibility was a teaching position in South America. She reasoned that, having delayed her vocation in deference to her mother, her mother would probably be happier with a daughter in a German convent than teaching in a foreign land thousands of miles away. She applied to the Cologne Carmel and was interviewed there on May 20, 1933, entered with them on October 14 of that year and was accepted as a novice six months later, becoming Sister Teresa Benedicta of the Cross.

While at the Cologne Carmel she continued her scholarship, finishing her finest philosophical work *Finite and Eternal Being*. She was finally professed there in 1938, but within a few months she fled Nazi Germany to the Echt Carmel in Holland. Holland was safe only for a few years, and by 1942 Edith was seeking permission to move to the French-speaking Carmel at Le Paquier, Switzerland. Official paperwork, from Holland, Switzerland, and Rome, delayed her and when, one Sunday afternoon in August, 1942, two SS officers asked to see her at the Echt Carmel, the superior assumed they were there to process her emigration.

They gave her five minutes to pack her things.

The Netherlands Red Cross report states that she was killed "For reasons of race and specifically because of Jewish descent." She was Number 44074: Edith Theresia Hedwig Stein, Echt.

The selection below is neither characteristic of her phenomenological research nor of her spiritual writing, yet it combines the outlook of each. It is, however, characteristic of her understanding of the place of women in the world. Woman as healer need not be restrained by the ordinary roles of men and women, for women may equally be united to the humanity of Christ through the mystery of the Cross. Such union can only come about if the individual is "present, by the power of His Cross, at every front, every place of sorrow, bringing to those who suffer comfort, healing, and salvation."

From *Essays on Women*

A quality unique to woman is her singular sensitivity to moral values and an abhorrence of all which is low and mean; this quality protects her against the dangers of seduction and of total surrender to sensuality. This is expressed by the mysterious prophecy, become legendary, that woman would be engaged in battle against the serpent; and this prophecy is fulfilled by the victory over evil won for all humanity through Mary, queen of all women. Allied closely to this sensitivity for moral values is her yearning for the divine and for her own personal union with the Lord, her readiness and desire to be completely fulfilled and guided by His love. That is why, in a rightly-ordered family life, the mission of moral and religious education is given chiefly to the wife. If her life is anchored completely in Jesus, then, also, she is best protected against the dangerous loss of moderation. This could happen by her being overly wrapped-up in those about her; or, on the contrary, it could happen by her being wrapped up only in herself and would cut the ground from under her feet, the ground on which she must stand if she is to be able to support and to help others. Her professional activity counterbalances the risk of submerging herself all too intimately in another's life and thereby sacrificing her own; however, an exclusive preoccupation with her professional activity would bring the opposite danger of infidelity toward her feminine vocation. Only those who surrender themselves completely into the Lord's hands can trust that they will avoid disaster between Scylla and Charybdis. Whatever is surrendered to Him is not lost but it saved, chastened, exalted and proportioned out in true measure.

We are led by these last comments to the question of the vocation practised outside of the home and of the relationship between man and woman in professional life. Obviously now, because of the development of the last decades and of recent years, we must consider as closed the historical epoch which made an absolute differentiation between the duties of the sexes, i.e., that woman should assume the domestic duties and man the struggle for a livelihood. Today, it is not at all too difficult for us to understand how this evolution took place. The victories of natural science and technology which progressively replaced human labor by mechanical means brought to women a great liberation and a desire to use their nascent powers in another way. In the transitional period, much unused power was senselessly squandered in empty dawdling; and, because of this, valuable human energy was wasted away. The necessary changes were brought about only after a series of difficult crises. These crises were partly caused through excessive passion, both on the part of the pioneers of the feminist movement and of their opponents, although they both often fought with humane arguments. In part, these crises were caused by the passive opposition of the inert multitude which tends to cling without objective scrutiny to the accustomed ways of the past. At last, post-war conditions in Germany brought revolutionary changes even in this domain; and the accompanying economic depression compelled even those who until then had had no thoughts of professional training to work for a living. Hence, the condition in which we find ourselves today is an abnormal one, and it does not constitute a suitable basis for fundamental analysis.

Above all, with regard to the previous explanation, we must ask: On the whole does woman's professional life outside of the home violate the order of nature and grace? I believe that one must answer "no" to this question. It seems to me that a common creativity in all areas was assigned in the original order, even if this was with a differing allocation of roles. The change in the original order which took place after the Fall does not signify its complete termination; thus nature also was not fully corrupted but preserved the same powers, only now weakened and exposed to error. The fact that *all* powers which the husband possesses are present in a feminine nature as well—even though they may generally appear in different degrees and relationships—is an indication they should be employed in corresponding activity. And wherever the circle of domestic duties is too narrow for the wife to attain the full formation of her powers, both nature and reason concur that she reach out beyond this circle. It appears to me, however, that there is a limit to such professional activities whenever it jeopardizes domestic life, i.e., the community of life and formation consisting of parents and children. It even seems to me a contradiction of the divine order when the professional activities of the husband escalate to a degree which cuts him off completely from family life. This is even more true of the wife. Any social condition is an unhealthy one which compels married women to seek gainful employment and makes it impossible for them to manage their home. And we should accept as normal that the married woman is restricted to domestic life at a time when her household duties exact her total energies.

After the Fall, woman was forced to care for the most primitive necessities of life, which resulted in a severe curtailment of her powers; in this respect, she has benefited from conditions brought about by cultural change. Moreover, the change in her destiny implied her subordination to man: the extent and type of her activity were made dependent on his will; and, because his judgment and will are not infallible, she is not guaranteed that his control over her will be regulated by right reason. Moreover, inasmuch as the harmony between the sexes was disordered by the Fall, the question of the subordination of woman involved a bitter conflict concerning the activities suitable to corrupted masculine as well as feminine nature.

The redemptive order restores the original relationship; the more redemption is personally adopted, the more it makes possible a harmonious collaboration and an agreement concerning the allotment of vocational roles. It caused a further basic change in the status of woman by asserting the ideal of virginity. This broke through the Old Testament norm which stipulates that woman effects her salvation only by bearing children. And in those particular cases where individual women like Deborah and Judith had been called divinely to extraordinary achievements for God's people, even the norm of the Old Covenant had been changed as well. Now a new way reveals that women can consecrate themselves exclusively to the service of God, and they can develop a manifold activity in His service. Even the same St. Paul whose writings so often strongly echo Old Testament views has pronounced clearly that, from his point of view, it is good for men as well as for women to marry but it may be better not to marry. And now and then, he emphasizes the praiseworthy achievement of women in the service of the first pastoral communities (1 Cor 6).

Before considering men and women's common vocation in God's service, we would like to consider the problem of the distribution of vocations according to the natural order. Should certain positions be reserved only for men, others for only women, and perhaps a few open for both? I believe that this question also must be answered negatively. The strong individual differences existing within both sexes must be taken into account. Many women have masculine characteristics just as many men share feminine ones. Consequently, every so-called "masculine" occupation may be exercised by many women as well as many "feminine" occupations by certain men.

It seems right, therefore, that no legal barriers of any kind should exist. Rather, one can hope that a natural choice of vocation may be made thanks to an upbringing, education, and guidance in harmony with the individual's nature; unsuitable elements should be eliminated by strict objective requirements. The differences between masculine and feminine natures indicate clearly that a specific aptitude for certain professions is present in each. Thus, the choice of a profession will usually resolve itself.

Dorothy Day (1897–1980)

Dorothy Day came from the heart of America, and spent her life chastisting it. Her father's family came from the corner where Georgia meets Tennessee, her grandfather having been a Confederate army surgeon. Her mother and those before her came from the Northeast, from the upper Hudson Valley and from Massachusetts. They were Episcopalians. They were whalers, chairmakers, boat captains, and parents of large families. Her own father was a newspaperman, and she inherited a recognition of the power of the word. They lived in Brooklyn and in California and in Chicago, where she eventually went to college after having finished high school at the age of sixteen.

She worked as a writer, was jailed in Washington, D.C., for participating in an anti-war demonstration, and worked during 1918 as a nurse at Kings County Hosptial in Brooklyn. Later she worked as a writer for the *Liberator*, the successor to *The Masses*, and entered into a common law marriage with Forster Batterham, with whom she had one daughter.

Dorothy Day was radical. She probably was "a radical," but the more important term for her is simply radical. She was radical in her belief, she was radical in her poverty, she was radical in her devotion to the church. She is hard to characterize because her life was so characteristic of what we think of as "Christian" that it seems as if we are painting a caricature. Her absolute and complete self-donation to God through her absolute commitment to others, singly, one by one, is more readily apparent by her small actions than by her larger ones.

She baptized her baby and abandonded Forster when he would not or could not share her newfound Catholicism. She began to live even more radically, living and working with the poor. With Peter Maurin she founded The Catholic Worker Movement, a lay apostolate imbedded in and representative of the principal of subsidiarity—decentralized, cooperative, and communal decision-making and work. It has Houses of Hospitality in over sixty United States cities along with several communal farms in various parts of the country.

The Movement itself promotes pacifism and voluntary poverty, and the hallmark of both the Movement and the Houses of Hospitality is inclusiveness and respect: no one is to be made to feel like an outsider. They used the term "personalism" to mean personal activism—charity is much more than running a shelter or writing a check—and those whom you serve are "ambassadors of God" who give you the opportunity to serve. The corporal works of mercy, she knew, are useless without the spiritual works of mercy. *The Catholic Worker*, a small tabloid newspaper begun in 1933, presents the news and interests, and spreads the concept of The Catholic Worker Movement. There is an aloneness to her commitment to others that is echoed in the title of her autobiography, *The Long Loneliness*. But she was as single-minded as Mary Ward, from whom she took the phrase.

Dorothy Day saw most clearly the connection between social justice and peace. In the selection below, from her book *Loaves and Fishes*, she describes voluntary poverty both as a means of understanding human dignity and as a way to recognize complete and utter dependence upon God.

From *Loaves and Fishes*

Chapter 8
A Baby Is Always Born with a Loaf of Bread Under Its Arm

This was the consoling remark my brother's Spanish mother-in-law used to make when a new baby was about to arrive. It is this philosophy which makes it possible for people to endure a life of poverty.

"Just give me a chance," I hear people say. "Just let me get my debts paid. Just let me get a few things I need and then I'll begin to think of poverty and its rewards. Meanwhile, I've had nothing but." But these people do not understand the difference between inflicted poverty and voluntary poverty; between being the victims and the champions of poverty. I prefer to call the one kind *destitution*, reserving the word *poverty* for what St. Francis called "Lady Poverty."

We know the misery being poor can cause. St. Francis was "the little poor man" and none was more joyful than he; yet Francis began with tears, in fear and trembling, hiding out in a cave from his irate father. He appropriated some of his father's goods (which he considered his rightful inheritance) in order to repair a church and rectory where he meant to live. It was only later that he came to love Lady Poverty. Perhaps kissing the leper was the great step that freed him not only from fastidiousness and a fear of disease but from attachment to worldly goods as well.

It is hard to advocate poverty when a visitor tells you how he and his family lived in a basement room and did sweatshop work at night to make ends meet, then how the landlord came in and abused them for not paying promptly his exorbitant rent.

It is hard to advocate poverty when the back yard at Chrystie Street still has the furniture piled to one side that was put out on the street in a recent eviction from a tenement next door.

How can we say to such people, "Be glad and rejoice, for your reward is very great in Heaven," especially when we are living comfortably in a warm house and sitting down to a good table, and are clothed warmly? I had occasion to visit the City Shelter last month, where homeless families are cared for. I sat there for a couple of hours contemplating poverty and destitution in a family. Two of the children were asleep in the parents' arms and four others were sprawling against them. Another young couple were also waiting, the mother pregnant. I did not want to appear to be spying, since all I was there for was the latest news on apartment-finding possibilities for homeless families. So I made myself known to the young man in charge. He apologized for having let me sit there; he'd thought, he explained, that I was "just one of the clients."

Sometimes, as in St. Francis' case, freedom from fastidiousness and detachment from worldly things, can be attained in only one step. We would like to think this is often so. And yet the older I get the more I see that life is made up of many steps, and they are very small ones, not giant strides. I have "kissed a leper" not once but twice—consciously—yet I cannot say I am much the better for it.

The first time was early one morning on the steps of Precious Blood Church. A woman with cancer of the face was begging (beggars are allowed only in slums), and when I gave her money—which was no sacrifice on my part but merely passing on alms someone had given me—she tried to kiss my hand. The only thing I could do was to kiss her dirty old face with the gaping hole in it where an eye and a nose had been. It sounds like a heroic deed, but it was not. We get used to ugliness so quickly. What we avert our eyes from today can be borne tomorrow when we have learned a little more about love. Nurses know this, and so do mothers.

The second time I was refusing a bed to a drunken prostitute with a huge, toothless, rouged mouth, a nightmare of a mouth. She had been raising a disturbance in the house. I kept remembering how St. Thérèse of Lisieux said that when you had to say no, when you had to refuse anyone anything, you could at least do it so that the person went away a bit happier. I had to deny this woman a bed, and when she asked me to kiss her I did, and it was a loathsome thing, the way she did it. It was scarcely a mark of normal human affection.

We suffer these things and they fade from memory. But daily, hourly, to give up our own possessions and especially to subordinate our own impulses and wishes to others—these are hard, hard things; and I don't think they ever get any easier.

You can strip yourself, you can be stripped, but still you will reach out like an octopus to seek your own comfort, your untroubled time, your ease, your refreshment. It may mean books or music—gratification of the inner senses—or it may mean food and drink, coffee and cigarettes. The one kind of giving up is no easier than the other.

Occasionally—often after reading the life of such a saint as Benedict Joseph Labre—we start thinking about poverty, about going out alone, living with the destitute, sleeping on park benches or in the city shelter, living in churches, sitting before the Blessed Sacrament as we see so many doing who come from the municipal lodging house or the Salvation Army around the corner. And when such thoughts come on warm spring days, when children are playing in the park and it is good to be out on the city streets, we know that we are only deceiving ourselves: for we are only dreaming of a form of luxury. What we want is the warm sun, and rest, and time to think and read, and freedom from the people who press in on us from early morning until late at night. No, it is not simple, this business of poverty.

Over and over again in the history of the Church the saints have emphasized voluntary poverty. Every religious community, begun in poverty and incredible hardship, but with a joyful acceptance of hardship by the rank-and-file priests, brothers, monks, or nuns who gave their youth and energy to good works, soon began to "thrive." Property was extended until holdings and buildings accumulated; and, although there is still individual poverty in the community, there is corporate wealth. It is hard to remain poor.

One way to keep poor is not to accept money which comes from defrauding the poor. Here is a story of St. Ignatius of Sardinia, a Capuchin recently canonized. Ignatius used to go out from his monastery with a sack to beg from the people of the town, but he would never go to a certain merchant who had built his fortune by defrauding the poor. Franchine, the rich man, fumed every time the saint passed his door. His concern, however, was not the loss of the opportunity to give alms but fear of public opinion. He complained at the friary, whereupon the Father Guardian ordered St. Ignatius to beg from the merchant the next time he went out.

"Very well," said Ignatius obediently. "If you wish it, Father, I will go, but I would not have the Capuchins dine on the blood of the poor."

The merchant received Ignatius with great flattery and gave him generous alms, asking him to come again in the future. But, as Ignatius was leaving the house with his sack on his shoulder, drops of blood began oozing from the sack. They trickled down on Franchine's doorstep and ran down through the street to the monastery. Everywhere Ignatius went a trail of blood followed him.

When he arrived at the friary, he laid the sack at the Father Guardian's feet. "Here," Ignatius said, "is the blood of the poor."

This story appeared in the last column written by a great Catholic layman, a worker for social justice, F. P. Kenkel, editor of *Social Justice Review* in St. Louis (and always a friend of Peter Maurin's).

Mr. Kenkel's comment was that the universal crisis in the world today was created by love of money. "The Far East and the Near East [and he might have said all Latin America and Africa also] together constitute a great sack from which blood is oozing. The flow will not stop as long as our interests in these people are dominated largely by financial and economic considerations."

This and other facts seem to me to point more strongly than ever to the importance of voluntary poverty today. At least we can avoid being comfortable through the exploitation of others. And at least we can avoid physical wealth as the result of a war economy. There may be ever-improving standards of living in the United States, with every worker eventually owning his own home and driving his own car; but our whole modern economy is based on preparation for war, and this surely is one of the great arguments for poverty in our time. If the comfort one achieves results in the death of millions in the future, then that comfort shall be duly paid for. Indeed, to be literal, contributing to the war (misnamed "defense") effort is very difficult to avoid. If you work in a textile mill making cloth, or in a factory making dungarees or blankets, your work is still tied up with war. If you raise food or irrigate the land to raise food, you may be feeding troops or liberating others to serve as troops. If you ride a bus you are paying taxes. Whatever you buy is taxed, so that you are, in effect, helping to support the state's preparations for war exactly to the extent of your attachment to worldly things of whatever kind.

The act and spirit of giving are the best counter to the evil forces in the world today, and giving liberates the individual not only spiritually but materially. For, in a world enslavement through installment buying and mortgages, the only way to live in any true security is to live so close to the bottom that when you fall you do not have far to drop, you do not have much to lose.

And in a world of hates and fears, we can look to Peter Maurin's words for the liberation that love brings: "Voluntary poverty is the answer. We cannot see our brother in need without stripping ourselves. It is the only way we have of showing our love."

Jessica Powers (1905–1988)

Jessica Powers was born on February 7, 1905 in Mauston, Wisconsin and died on August 18, 1988 at the Carmel of the Mother of God, Pewaukee, Wisconsin. She lived a life writ in silence and in joyful, lyric poetry. She wrote nearly four hundred poems and hundreds of letters, many of which survive in private collections and university archives.

Her grandparents emigrated from Ireland to Wisconsin, where she was born the third of four children of John and Delia Trainer Powers. Her older sister, Dorothy, died when Jessica was eleven. Her father died two years later, the spring before she began attending high school. After high school she enrolled in the Marquette University school of journalism (the school of liberal arts did not accept women then), but left after one year and worked as a secretary in Chicago while feeding her love of poetry with reading in libraries.

Jessica's mother died when she was twenty, and she returned to the family farm, keeping house until her brothers John and Daniel married. She wrote poetry, which began to appear in local papers, and she contributed a column entitled "The Percolator" to *The Milwaukee Sentinel*. She left the farm in 1936, first going to Chicago and then, in 1937, to New York, where she entered into the Catholic literary circle that included Jessie and Anton Pegis, with whom she lived. Her first book of poems, *The Lantern Burns*, was published in New York in 1939. It contains some of her best work, including "The Master Beggar," a deep evocation of her call to complete self-donation, apparently as an apostolic religious.

But Jessica found her vocation in contemplative life. In 1941, at age thirty-six, she entered the Milwaukee Carmel.

There she became Sister Miriam of the Holy Spirit, and was perpetually professed in 1946, the same year in which her second book of poems, *The Place of Splendor,* was published. Four additional books of poetry, *The Little Alphabet* (1955), *Mountain Sparrow* (1972), *Journey to Bethlehem* (1980), and *The House at Rest* (1984) preceded the *Selected Poetry of Jessica Powers,* from which the poems below are taken.

Her life in Carmel was often busy. She was elected prioress three times, in 1955, in 1958, and in 1964, and supervised its move from Milwaukee to Pewaukee in 1958. She was in a tuberculosis sanatorium for one year, October 1959 to October 1960, and returned to her duties as prioress shortly after the new year, 1961, when she wrote: "I have been so busy being Martha that I have no Mary thoughts at all." As her second term came toward its end, she wrote again: "My six-year term is up as Prioress, so there will necessarily be changes. I am so happy to have the good shelter of obedience again and to lead a life of simplicity—I was going to say, free from care, but who knows?"

In all, six books of poetry by Jessica Powers were published, either privately or by small presses, but she barely wrote at all while serving as Prioress. The five poems below are windows to her life with God: the first three move from vocation to renunciation to understanding; the latter two are born of her experience as prioress. She encourages the reader to pass through the "Pure Desert" of difficult prayer; her advice is reflected in an earlier letter: "In spite of the dealings I have had with souls I know that it is difficult to discern what is a temporary sandstorm blinding one's vision, with clear blue air beyond, and what is hopeless desert waste which one will most likely succumb to, 'no way and no water' anywhere." The last poem here, "Total Virgin," can be read both as her speaking of another and as our understanding of the life of Jessica Powers.

She maintained a lively and deeply spiritual correspondence with many persons, including Sr. Margaret Ellen

Traxler, S.S.N.D., founder of the Institute of Women Today in Chicago, from whose papers the letter selections,
above and below, are taken.

The Master Beggar

Worse than the poorest mendicant alive,
the pencil man, the blind man with his breath
of music shaming all who do not give,
are You to me, Jesus of Nazareth.

Must You take up Your post on every block
of every street? Do I have no release?
Is there no room of earth that I can lock
to Your sad face, Your pitiful whisper "Please"?

I seek the counters of time's gleaming store
but make no purchases, for You are there.
How can I waste one coin while you implore
with tear-soiled cheeks and dark blood-matted hair?

And when I offer You in charity
pennies minted by love, still, still You stand
fixing Your sorrowful wide eyes on me.
Must all my purse be emptied in Your hand?

Jesus, my beggar, what would You have of me?
Father and mother? the lover I longed to know?
The child I would have cherished tenderly?
Even the blood that through my heart's valves flow?

I too would be a beggar. Long tormented,
I dream to grant You all and stand apart
with You on some bleak corner, tear-frequented,
and trouble mankind for its human heart.

                    (1937)

Having Renounced You

Having tonight renounced you utterly,
and bending low to lay hope in a tomb

that needs no trusty guard lest there be
a subsequent resurrection, making room
across my lands for the long evening,
still have I joy so positive I sing.

For now there is no finger of possession
upon my prayers for you, and when I go
into God's presence with the bleak confession
He will be moved with pity as I stand
holding that master weapon in my hand.

(1938; 1939)

God Is a Strange Lover

God is the strangest of all lovers; His ways are past explaining.
He sets His heart on a soul; He says to Himself, "Here will
                              I rest My love."
But He does not woo her with flowers or jewels or words that
                              are set to music,
no names endearing, no kindled praise His heart's direction
                              prove.
His jealousy is an infinite thing. He stalks the soul
                              with sorrows;
He tramples the bloom; He blots the sun that could make
                              her vision dim.
He robs and breaks and destroys—there is nothing at last but
                              her own shame, her own affliction,
and then He comes and there is nothing in the vast world but
                              Him and her love of Him.

Not till the great rebellions die and her will is safe in His
                              hands forever
does He open the door of light and His tendernesses fall,
and then for what is seen in the soul's virgin places,
for what is heard in the heart, there is no speech at all.

God is a strange lover; the story of His love is most surprising.
There is no proud queen in her cloth of gold; over and over again

there is only, deep in the soul, a poor disheveled woman
    weeping . . .
for us who have need of a picture and words: the Magdalen.

(1947;1984)

Pure Desert

"The more one runs in the spiritual life
    the less tired one gets."—Padre Pio

This is pure Gobi desert, you declare;
I see, past sandstorms (of exaggeration)
and rage of flesh at ghostly motivation,
pink health invade your prayer.

Pure desert, you complain, though now you walk
who once had shuffled through the arid miles.
Sighting a day of flight, I shelve my smiles
and share your pilgrim talk.

All true ascesis as a desert lies:
hot wind, hot sand, no water, and no way.
The ego agonizes through each day.
Freedom is when it dies.

I coax you onward: soon, first breeze of bliss;
soon, sun that scorches cooled to sun that warms.
Your youth will dance when shady lanes lock arms
with each green oasis.

(1961; 1984)

Total Virgin
"She was virgin even of herself."—Pere Francois, O.C.D.

In a house of mirrors that coveted her image
she never walked
with her own beauty
nor made a feast of her goodness,

inviting friends from the far and wide.
She never sat down with her own innocence
to dialogue together,
nor called a stranger in
to sit at her hearth and be glorified.

She was a maiden promised to one lover
whom she was always seeking.
Though he hid in her heartbeat and settled himself
behind her breath,
he was distance, too. Journeys dwindled to places
beside her own, and miles melted beneath
her steps of wanting. She could by-pass all
meadows that trap us with their poisonous flowers
and their soliciting pools
and winding lanes that skirt the only death.

She was out on a road alone, hastening onward,
gathering all as gift, the small and great
fragments of mystery and reality.
Everything was for Him, even her own being.
Since love marks neither measurement or weight
she carried all, without touching or tasting.

Life which comes as a virgin to us all,
most safely came to her.
Time, when she passed, remained inviolate.

(1976; 1984)

February 3, 1963

When I was a novice, my Mistress gave me Caussade to read for
our Spiritual Reading after Vespers, and because I did not speak
of it never offered to give me another book for that time, so for
two years Caussade was my spiritual nourishment; I know much
of him by heart. In that I see God's will, for I am grateful for
that spiritual formation on abandonment. Not that I have ever
really practiced abandonment in that perfect degree, but the prin-

ciples of it are in my mind. His peace and recollection are a thing
to aim for. I read a sentence the other day that I like: "The memory of God that is based on recollection is a spiritual resurrection." Would that all souls could be "raised from the dead" to
live in the presence of God. It would cure all the ills in the world.

Does it not seem to you . . . that we are entering a new wonderful age, of spiritual renewal and transformation in the Church?
We are suddenly aware of our great obligations of Christian charity, and there seems to be a great flowering of truth and love.
Out of this Vatican Council one expects a new surge of life in
the Church.

August 22, 1973

I am studying St. John of the Cross again and love the ideal of
union with God to which he urges us. The escape from self-love.
It is like new inspiration. Don't you think life has a number of
calls—here and there a new "Go forth" like Abraham's. And we
tear up our roots and go.

December 16, 1976

Life happens, someone said, while you are making other plans.
How often we go where we did not expect to go.

June 20, no year

. . . I don't want to say too much along this line, because it
sounds neurotic to claim unworthiness, but I want to say at least
once dear Sister Margaret Ellen who have been such a joy to me
with your beautiful love, that I am indeed a poor little creature
and I never felt it so clearly as the Sunday you came. My poverty became infinite.

First of all, it was so difficult to talk about prayer. I do not
know if I pray at all; I just live with Our Lord. All I could think
of to describe prayer was to live in His presence as *offered*, because I think prayer is, as St. Therese said of holiness, a disposition of the heart. It is loving Him and wanting to please Him and
if words are needed, fine, but if there are no words but just the
love and desire of Him then it seems as if that is enough. Christ
is with us and gives meaning to everything that happens and
everything that we see or hear, and there is an immense joy in

everything because He has arranged it so. I know He has not "arranged" the evil, but He made an imperfect world, and He lived with it and suffered with it, and it is privilege to share it all with Him. Someone has said we do not save others by changing and correcting and developing them; we redeem them by the love that accepts them and serves them as they are. Jesus did not make much of a dent on the society of his own time. It is what He is, what we are that produces the harvest—after the seed has fallen into the ground. Caussade said that prayer was just carrying peace in one's heart, but I would add: with a sense (even not adverted to) that the peace came from God and it is His. Or prayer is going through the day filled with thanksgiving. Or filled with praise. Or humbled in His sight, but with an undercurrent of joy and the rightness of it all. Or just a longing in one's heart for Christ and His kingdom. Or a sense of complete and loving surrender to what He has chosen (or seems to have chosen—sometimes it is so difficult to be sure what God really want[s] us to do—submit or resist, endure or rebel—because sometimes God wants us to rebel, doesn't He?) Our Holy Mother said that prayer was not so much thinking as loving, so I suppose prayer is actually loving God through all the changing events and emotions of our lives. I do not think one needs very man[y] words for love, but surely one would find expressions of love at times. Of course, there should be formal and community prayer.

. . . There seems to be a new interest in prayer and the interior life. Even in distorted forms—the young who refuse to go to Mass but will dabble in eastern mysticism or psychedelic "trips" and queer goings-on. Not that everyone wasn't always interested, but it seems that the interest is keener now, when we see that the material values and laws and norms and the old structures have failed us.

. . . Do forgive me for all this expounding. . . . It sounds as if I were giving you a treatise on prayer, -no. You asked me about prayer and I just wanted to tell you my ideas in answer. I am sure you have a BEAUTIFUL prayer life because you give yourself to others, and with such gracious love.

Simone Weil (1909-1943)

Simone Weil is probably one of the best published enigmas of this century. She was convinced of Catholicism, but never baptized. She was trained as an intellectual, but wrote from the heart. She was rooted in the dignity of the person, but died of self-starvation.

The parameters of her life, from her birth in Paris on February 3, 1909 to her death in Kent, England on August 29, 1943, encompass two ruptures of world peace. She was, unquestionably, a philosophical genius who excelled in her academic work and who became a public champion of the ideals she saw embedded in Christianity. Her very brief adult life was marked by internal and external identification with the plight of the worker, from her solidarity with the unemployed workers at Le Puy, where she taught in 1932, to her working in the fields of Jura soon after, to her working in the Renault factory. In the summer of 1936 she traveled to Spain to see firsthand the conflict between the communists and the supporters of Francesco Franco, and it is there she experienced the reality of war. She traveled, to Portugal and to Italy, and knelt for the first time in 1937 at Santa Maria degli Angeli in Assisi: "something stronger than I compelled me for the first time in my life to go down on my knees."

She moved from Paris to the port city of Marseilles in October, 1940, and some months later met the Dominican Father Joseph M. Perrin (b. 1905) who encouraged her and engaged her in philosophical conversation while she continued to share a worker's life of manual labor. Fr. Perrin became Prior of the Dominican Convent at Montpelier, so their conversations continued in letters. It was to him she wrote her spiritual autobiography, in which she presented her argument for not being baptized: "a genuine vocation might prevent anyone from entering the Church." For her, intellectual purity required she remain the outsider.

She was of Jewish descent, but had no familial religious upbringing or support. Marxism fascinated her for a while, and her insistence on sharing common poverty moved from that base to a Christian base apparently without recognizing that the freedom to *choose* poverty in no way identifies one with the poor.

A part of her refusal to be baptized could rest in her understanding of how deeply religion is rooted in the psyche, and the fact that so often changes in religion come from a need for external comfort rather than internal commitment. As she writes below, "A change of religion is for the soul like a change of language for the writer." Since she had no religion to speak of, her deep attraction to Christ, Eucharist, and the Gospel might have eventually overcome her social, philosophical, and historical objections to Christianity. She was, for her brief life, continually engaged in the arduous, and occasionally joyful, task of "waiting for God."

Her writings—predominantly fragments, journal notes, essays, and letters—have been collected, edited, and published in various volumes by Father Perrin and Gustave Thibon, who have written the definitive biography of her life. Her intellectual quests and her emotional searches eventually fused in her recognition of Eucharist as the ultimate expression of truth. What follows is a selection from the essay "The Love of Religious Practices" from *Waiting for God*.

From *Waiting for God*

The Love of Religious Practices

The love of institutional religion, although the name of God necessarily comes into it, is not in itself an explicit, but an implicit love of God, for it does not involve direct, immediate contact with him. God is present in religious practices, when they are pure, just as he is present in our neighbor and in the beauty of the world; in the same way and not any more.

The form that the love of religion takes in the soul differs a great deal according to the circumstances of our lives. Some circumstances prevent the very birth of this love; others kill it before it has been able to grow very strong. In affliction some men, in spite of themselves, develop a hatred and contempt for religion because the cruelty, pride, or corruption of certain of its ministers have made them suffer. There are others who have been reared from their earliest youth in surroundings impregnated with a spirit of this sort. We must conclude that in such cases, by God's mercy, the love of our neighbor and the love of the beauty of the world, if they are sufficiently strong and pure, will be enough to raise the soul to any height.

The love of institutional religion normally has as its object the prevailing religion of the country or circle in which a man is brought up. As the result of an inborn habit, everyone thinks first of that each time he thinks of a religious service.

The whole virtue of religious practices can be conceived of from the Buddhist tradition concerning the recitation of the name of the Lord. It is said that Buddha made a vow to raise to himself, in the Land of Purity, all those who pronounced his name with the desire of being saved by him; and that because of this vow the recitation of the name of the Lord really has the power of transforming the soul.

Religion is nothing else but this promise of God. Every religious practice, every rite, all liturgy is a form of the recitation of the name of the Lord and in principle should have a real virtue, the virtue of saving whoever devotes himself to performing it with desire.

All religions pronounce the name of God in their particular language. As a rule it is better for a man to name God in his native tongue rather than in one that is foreign to him. Except in special cases the soul is not able to abandon itself utterly when it has to make the slight effort of seeking for the words in a foreign language, even when this language is well known.

A writer whose native language is poor, difficult to manipulate, and not widely known throughout the world is very strongly tempted to adopt another. There are a few like Conrad who have done so with startling success. But they are very rare. Except in special cases such a change does harm, both thought and style suffer, the writer is always ill at ease in the adopted language and cannot rise above mediocrity.

A change of religion is for the soul like a change of language for a writer. All religions, it is true, are not equally suitable for the recitation of the name of the Lord. Some, without any doubt, are very imperfect mediums. The religion of Israel, for instance, must have been imperfect when it made the crucifixion of Christ possible. The Roman religion can scarcely be said to deserve the name of religion at all.

But in general the relative value of the various religions is a very difficult thing to discern; it is almost impossible, perhaps quite impossible. For a religion is known only from inside. Catholics say this of Catholicism, but it is true of all religions. Religion is a form of nourishment. It is difficult to appreciate the flavor and food value of something one has never eaten.

The comparison of religions is only possible, in some measure, through the miraculous virtue of sympathy. We can know men to a certain extent if at the same time as we observe them from outside we manage by sympathy to transport our own soul into theirs for a time. In the same way the study of different religions does not lead to a real knowledge of them unless we transport ourselves for a time by faith to the very center of whichever one we are studying. Here, moreover, this word faith is used in its strongest sense.

This scarcely ever happens, for some have no faith, and the others have faith exclusively in one religion and only bestow upon the others the sort of attention we give to strangely shaped shells. There are others again who think they are capable of impartiality because they have only a vague religiosity which they can turn indifferently in any direction, whereas, on the contrary, we must have given all our attention, all our faith, all our love to a particular religion in order to think of any other religion with the high degree of attention, faith, and love that is proper to it. In the same way, only those who are capable of friendship can take a real heartfelt interest in the fate of an utter stranger.

In all departments of life, love is not real unless it is directed toward a particular object; it becomes universal without ceasing to be real only as a result of analogy and transference.

It might be said in passing that the knowledge of what analogy and transference are, a knowledge for which mathematics, the various branches of science, and philosophy are a preparation, also has a direct relationship to love.

In Europe today, and perhaps even in the whole world, the knowledge of comparative religion amounts to just about nothing. People have not even a notion of the possibility of such a knowledge. Even without the prejudices which get in our way, it is already very difficult for us even to form an idea of it. Among the different forms of religion there are, as it were, partial compensations for the visible differences, certain hidden equivalents which can only be caught sight of by the most penetrating discernment. Each religion is an original combination of explicit and implicit truths; what is explicit in one is implicit in another. The implicit adherence to a truth can in some cases be worth as much as the explicit adherence, sometimes even a great deal more. He who knows the secrets of all hearts alone knows the secret of the different forms of faith. He has never revealed this secret, whatever anyone may say.

If one is born into a religion which is not too unsuitable for pronouncing the name of the Lord, if one loves this native religion with a well directed and pure love, it is difficult to imagine a legitimate motive for giving it up, before direct contact with God has placed the soul under the guidance of the divine will itself. After that the change is only legitimate if it is made in obedience. History shows that in fact this happens but rarely. Most often, perhaps always, the soul that has reached the highest realms of spirituality is confirmed in its love of the tradition that served it as a ladder.

If the imperfection of the religion in which one is born is too great, or if the form under which it appears in one's native surroundings is too corrupt, or if, through special circumstances, love for this religion has never been born or has been killed, the adoption of a foreign religion is legitimate. It is legitimate and necessary for certain people; probably not for everybody. This is the same with regard to those who have been brought up without the practice of any religion.

In all other cases, to change one's religion is a very serious decision, and it is much more serious to influence another person to change. It is yet more, infinitely more serious to exercise official pressure of such a nature in a conquered country.

On the other hand, in spite of all the varieties of religion existing in Europe and America, one might say that in principle, directly or indirectly, closely or only from afar, the Catholic religion forms the native spiritual background of all men belonging to the white races.

The virtue of religious practices is due to a contact with what is perfectly pure, resulting in the destruction of evil. Nothing here below is perfectly pure except the total beauty of the universe, and that we are unable to feel directly until we are very far advanced in the way of perfection. Moreover, this total beauty cannot be contained in anything tangible, though it is itself tangible in a certain sense.

Religious things are special tangible things, existing here below and yet perfectly pure. This is not on account of their own particular character. The church may be ugly, the singing out of tune, the priest corrupt, and the faithful inattentive. In a sense that is of no importance. It is as with a geometrician who draws a figure to illustrate a proof. If the lines are not straight and the circles are not round it is of no importance. Religious things are pure by right, theoretically, hypothetically, by convention. Therefore their purity is unconditioned. No stain can sully it. That is why it is perfect. It is not, however, perfect in the same way as Roland's mare, which, while it had all possible virtues, had also the drawback of not existing. Human conventions are useless if they are not connected with motives that impel people to observe them. In themselves they are simple abstractions; they are unreal and have no effect. But the convention by which religious things are pure is ratified by God himself. Thus it is an effective convention, a convention containing virtue and operating of itself. This purity is unconditioned and perfect, and at the same time real.

There we have a truth that is a fact and in consequence cannot be demonstrated by argument. It can only be verified experimentally.

It is a fact that the purity of religious things is almost everywhere to be seen in the form of beauty, when faith and love do not fail. Thus the words of the liturgy are marvelously beautiful; and the words of the prayer issued for us from the very lips of Christ is perfect above all. In the same way Romanesque architecture and Gregorian plain chant are marvelously beautiful.

At the very center, however, there is something utterly stripped of beauty, where there is no outward evidence of purity, something depending wholly on convention. It cannot be otherwise. Architecture, singing, language, even if the words are chosen by Christ himself, all those things are in a sense distinct from absolute purity. Absolute purity, present here below to our earthly senses, as a particular thing, such can only be a convention, which is a convention and nothing else. This convention, placed at the central point, is the Eucharist.

The virtue of the dogma of the real presence lies in its very absurdity. Except for the infinitely touching symbolism of food, there is nothing in a morsel of bread that can be associated with our thought of God. Thus the conventional character of the divine presence is evident. Christ can be present in such an object only by convention. For this very reason he can be perfectly present in it. God can only be present in secret here below. His presence in the Eucharist is truly secret since no part of our thought can reach the secret. Thus it is total.

Ita Ford (1940–1980)

Ita Ford was born in Brooklyn, N.Y. on April 23, 1940 and died forty years later, half a world away. After twelve years of Catholic schooling, she completed her education with a B.A. in English from Marymount Manhattan College. At twenty-one she entered the Maryknoll Sisters, a missionary community founded in this century. Nineteen years later, on December 2, 1980, she was murdered in El Salvador. She was shot at close range in the back of the head, and quite probably raped by one or more of the five guardsmen from the airport detachment of the El Salvador National Guard who crowded into the vehicle carrying her and her three companions and rode to a deserted crossroad at Hacienda San Francisco, several miles southwest of San Pedro Nonualco. With the murdered Maryknoll Sister Maura Clarke, Ursuline Sister Dorothy Kazel, and missionary Jean Donovan, she was buried in a shallow grave by villagers. The bodies were recovered and the two Maryknoll sisters, as is their custom, were later reinterred among the poor with whom they had worked and died.

Her life was one of patient listening and responding to the Lord. Three years after entering Maryknoll she left, after not being admitted to first vows. Disappointed but not broken, she worked as an editor for a religious publishing house. She rejoined Maryknoll in 1971 and made a "promise of fidelity" less than one year later. She completed a "Reflection Year" in 1978–79 in preparation for final commitment, but she wrote at the end of that year that her 1972 commitment was for life. She said she would be happy to make a final commitment on her return to Chile in the fall of 1979, but there is no evidence of her ever having done so.

The selections that follow show her ever mindful of the need to be certain of only one thing—a humble but active response to God. Her letter-present to her niece and godchild, Jennifer Sullivan, shows her dislike for aimlessness. The purpose one finds in life can only be ratified by God, but it is up to the individual to find and to maintain that purpose.

She spent most of her missionary life in Chile, but Ita Ford was riding in a jeep in El Salvador in August, 1980, when it was suddenly caught in a river torrent and overturned to the driver's side. She was pushed free by her close friend, Maryknoll Sister Carla Piette, who was driving and whose body was later recovered well downstream. She speaks of death, and of being a survivor in El Salvador, in the selections from letters to her mother and to Jean Bauman, a high school friend and life-long correspondent.

Her struggle was both personal and public. Her own life-long search is complimented by her call to help overcome the evils that restrained and restricted the people whom she served—the poor, abandoned, oppressed, and hopeless—from recognizing their own dignity and their ability to choose and to serve.

On note paper headed "Caminemos juntos sembrando flores de paz en nuestros caminos"

August 16, 1980

Dear Jennifer,

The odds that this note will arrive for your birthday are poor—but know I'm with you in spirit as you celebrate 16 big ones. I hope it's a special day for you.

I want to say something to you—& I wish I were there to talk to you—because sometimes letters don't get across all the meaning & feeling. But I'll give it a try anyway.

First of all, I love & care about you & how you are. I'm sure you know that. And that holds if you're an angel or a goof-off, a genius or a jerk. A lot of that is up to you & what you decide to do with your life.

What I want to say—some of it isn't too jolly birthday talk, but it's real. Yesterday I stood looking down at a 16 year old who had been killed a few hours earlier. I know a lot of kids even younger who are dead. This is a terrible time—El Salvador for youth. A lot of idealism and commitment is getting snuffed out here now.

The reasons why so many people are being killed are quite complicated—yet there are some clear, simple strands. One is that many people have found a meaning to live. So [they] sacrifice, struggle & even die! And whether their life spans 16 years or 60 or 90, for them their life has had a purpose. In many ways they are fortunate people.

Brooklyn is not passing through the drama of El Salvador—but some things hold true wherever one is—and at whatever age. What I'm saying is I hope you come to find that which gives life a deep meaning for you. Something worth living for—maybe even worth dying for—something that energizes you, enthuses you, enables you to keep moving ahead.

I can't tell you what it might be—that's for you to find, to choose, to love. I can just encourage you to start looking & support you in the search.

Maybe this sounds weird & off the wall—& maybe no one else will talk to you like this—but then, too, I'm seeing & living things that others around you aren't. And I also gather that you haven't been straining yourself this last year in school. Maybe you're into a drifting phase—I don't know. You or no one else have said. All I know is that I want to say to you—don't waste the gifts & opportunities you have to make yourself & other people happy. Do yourself & a lot of others a favor—get moving along.

I hope this doesn't sound like some kind of a sermon—because I don't mean it that way. Rather, its something that you learn here & I want to share it with you. In fact—it's my birthday present to you. If it doesn't make sense right at this moment, keep this & read it some time from now. Maybe it will be clearer. Or ask me about it. OK?

A very happy birthday to you & much, much love.

Ita

September 7, 1980

From a letter to her mother

. . . I know this is a very hard time for you. I know that you're concerned and worried about the situation and I don't know really how to alleviate that. I truly believe that I should be here and I can't even tell you why. A couple of weeks ago Carla and I were praying and we both cried because it was so unclear to us why we were here, although we felt strongly we should be. Well, it's now quite clear for Carla, but I still have to keep asking to be shown. I can't tell you not to worry—that would be unnatural—it would be like someone saying to me—don't hurt because Carla died. In fact the last few days have been really hurting ones—probably because the shock of the whole thing—the event and to my system—is wearing off. All I can share with you is that God's palpable presence has never been more real ever since we came to Salvador—He's made a lot of things clear to us—what we should be doing, etc.—and I trust in that and I hope you can too.

From a letter to Jean R. Baumann, high school friend

October 27, 1980

What can I say? Being a survivor isn't romantic or glorious. It's a bitch that you have to work through. Carla's death and my not dying when I thought I would is a lot to absorb & it takes time. I don't understand it, I don't like it—I have to humbly stand before the Lord & ask him to make sense of it since He's in charge. Meanwhile we keep plugging along because life is threatened by other evils worse than death—hatred, manipulation, vengeance, selfishness, etc. That's what we have to keep struggling against so that life-producing possibilities have a chance to flower.

Bibliography

Hildegard of Bingen

Hildegard of Bingen: Scivias. Trans. Columba Hart and Jane Bishop. New York: Paulist Press, 1990. BV5080.H5413 1990.

Scivias. Trans. Bruce Hozeski. Santa Fe: Bear, 1986. BV5080.H5413 1986.

Symphonia: A Critical Edition of the Symphonia Armonie Celestium Revelationum. Translations and commentary by Barbara Newman. Ithica, N.Y.: Cornell University Press, 1988. BV469.H534 S9513.

Beatrice of Nazareth

The Seven Steps of Love. Trans. Mary Josepha Carton, B.V.M. *Cistercian Studies* XIX:1 (1984).

Beguine Spirituality. Ed. Fiona Bowie, trans. Oliver Davies. New York: Crossroads, 1990.

Medieval Women's Visionary Literature. Ed. Elizabeth Alvida Petroff. New York: Oxford University Press, 1966.

Gertrude the Great

Exercises. Translated by a Benedictine Nun of Regina Laudis. Westminster, Md.: Newman Press, 1956. BV5080.G433.

The Herald of God's Loving Kindness. Trans. Alexandra Barratt. Kalamazoo: Cistercian Publications, 1991. BS2409.G4 L4314 1991.

Love, Peace, and Joy: A Month of the Sacred Heart According to St. Gertrude. Trans. Andre Prevot. Hales Corners, Wis.: Sacred Heart Monastery, 1911. BS2591.P7414 1911a.

O Beatatrinitas: The Prayers of St. Gertrude and St. Mechtilde.
Trans. John Gray. London: Sheed & Ward, 1927.
BX4700.G52B4 1927.
Spiritual Exercises: Gertrude the Great of Helfta. Trans. Gertrud
Jaron Lewis and Jack Lewis. Kalamazoo: Cistercian Publica-
tions, 1989.
BX2349.G42513 1989.

Julian of Norwich

*Juliana of Norwich: An Introductory Appreciation and an Inter-
pretative Anthology.* Ed. P. Franklin Chambers. London: Gol-
lancz, 1955.
BV4831.J78 1955.
Revelations of Divine Love. Ed. Grace Warrack. London:
Methuen, 1950.
BV4831.J8 1950.
A Shewing of God's Love. Edited and modernized by Sr. Anna
Maria Reynolds. New York: Longman's Press, 1958.
BV4831.F582.
Showings: Julian of Norwich. Trans. Edmund Colledge and James
Walsh. New York: Paulist Press, 1978.
BV4831.J8 1978.

Catherine of Siena

The Dialogue of the Seraphic Virgin. Trans. Algar Thorold. Lon-
don: K. Paul, Trench, Trubner, 1907.
920 C29.
The Dialogue. Trans. Suzanne Noffke. New York: Paulist Press,
1980.
BV5080.C2613 1980.
The Letters of Catherine of Siena. Trans. Suzanne Noffke. Bing-
hamton, N.Y.: Center for Medieval and Early Renaissance
Studies, State University of New York, 1988.
BX4700.C4 A4 1988.
The Orchard of Syon. Ed. Gabriel M. Liegey. New York: Ox-
ford University Press, 1966.
PR1119.A2 E64 no. 258.

Saint Catherine of Siena as Seen in Her Letters. Translated and edited by Vida D. Scudder. New York: E. P. Dutton, 1927. 920 C29s.

Teresa of Avila

The Collected Works of St. Teresa of Avila. Trans. Kieran Kavanaugh and Otilio Rodriguez. Washington: Institute for Carmelite Studies, 1976.
BX890.T353 1976.

The Complete Works of Saint Teresa of Jesus. Edited and translated by E. Allison Peers. London: Sheed & Ward, 1946.
BX890.T35 F46.

The Interior Castle or *The Mansions.* Ed., Hugh Martin. Trans. a Benedictine of Stanbrook. London: SCM Press, 1958.
BX2179.T4 M63 1958.

The Interior Castle. Trans. Kieran Kavanaugh and Otilio Rodriguez. New York: Paulist Press, 1979.
BX2179.T4 M63   1979.

The Letters of Saint Teresa of Jesus. Edited and translated by E. Allison Peers. London: Burns, Oates & Washburn, 1951.
920 T27L.

Libro de la vida: Santa Teresa de Jesus. Edicion de Damasco Chicharro. Madrid: Catedra, 1982.
BX4700.T4 A29   1982.

The Life of Teresa of Jesus: The Autobiography of St. Teresa of Avila. Edited and translated by E. Allison Peers. Garden City: Image Books, 1960.
920 T27L.

Obras Completas: Santa Teresa de Jesus, Madrid: Plenitud, 1964.
BX890.T35   1964.

Jane Frances de Chantal

Saint Jane Francis Frémyot de Chantal: Her Exhortations, Conferences and Instructions. Chicago: Loyola University Press, 1928.
BX2179.C4B7.

Selected Letters of Saint Jane Frances de Chantal. Trans. Sisters of the Visitation, Harrow-on-the-Hill. London: R & T. Washburn, 1918.
BV8311.H36 A2514   1918.

The Spiritual Life: A Summary of the Instructions on the Virtues and on Prayer Given by Saint Jane Frances Fremyot de Chantal. Compiled by the Sisters of the Visitation, Harrow-on-the Hill. London: Herder, 1928.
BV4630.C5.

Mary Ward

Till God Will: Mary Ward Through Her Writings. Ed. Emmanuel Orchard, I.B.V.M. London: Darton, Longman and Todd, 1985.
BX4705.W29W3   1985.

The Hidden Tradition: Women's Spiritual Writings Rediscovered. Ed. Lavinia Byrne. New York: Crossroad, 1991.

Jeanne Marie Guyon

Fénelon & Mme. Guyon: Documents Nouveaux et Inedits. Paris: Hachette, 1907.

Autobiography of Madame Guyon. Chicago: Christian Witness Co., 1910, c1880.

Justifications de la Doctrine de Madame de la Mothe-Guion. Paris: Ches les Libraires Associes, 1790.

Lettres Chretiennes et Spirituales. London, 1768.

Poesies et Cantiques Spirituels. Paris: Chez les Libraires Associes, 1790.

A Short Method of Prayer, and Spiritual Torrents, trans. the Paris edition of 1790 A. W. Marston. London: Samson Low, Marston, Low & Searle, 1875.

Elizabeth Seton

Elizabeth Seton: Selected Writings. Ed. Ellin M. Kelly and Annabelle M. Melville. New York: Paulist Press, 1987.
BX4700.S4 A3.

Letters of Mother Seton to Mrs. Julianna Scott. Ed. Joseph B. Code. New York: Father Salvator M. Burgio Memorial Foun-

dation in Honor of Mother Seton, 1960.
BV4375.S486 A257.

Edith Stein

Beitrage zur philosophischen Begrundung der Psychologie und der Geisteswissenschaften. Ein Untersuchung über den Staat. Tübingen: M. Niemeyer, 1970.
BF41.S7.
Essays on Women. Ed. L. Gelber and Romaeus Leuven. Trans. Freda Mary Uben. Washington: ICS Publications, 1987.
BQ7473.T43F7214   1987.
L'être fini et l'être éternel: essai d'un atteinte du sens de l'être. Louvain: Nauwelaerts, 1972.
BD331.S714M.
Life in a Jewish Family. Ed. L. Gelber and Romaeus Leuven. Trans. Josephine Koeppel. Washington: ICS Publications, 1986.
BV8392.T446   A2214   1986.
On the problem of empathy. Trans. Waltraut Stein. The Hague: M. Nijhoff, 1964.
BF575.E55 F64.
The Science of the Cross. A Study of St. John of the Cross. Ed. L. Gelber and Romaeus Leuven. Trans. Hilda Graef. London: Burns & Oates, 1960.
BQ7473.T43 K7414   1959.
Writings. Selected. Translated and introduced by Hilda Graef. Westminster: Newman Press, 1956.
BQ7473.T43 A4914   1956.

Dorothy Day

By Little and By Little: The Selected Writings of Dorothy Day. Ed. Robert Ellsberg. New York: Knopf, 1983.
HN37.C3 D385   1983.   Reprinted as *Dorothy Day: Selected Writings.* Ed. Robert Ellsberg. Maryknoll, N.Y.: Orbis Books, 1992.
From Union Square to Rome. New York: Arno Press, 1978.
BX4668.D3A32   1978.
House of Hospitality. New York: Sheed & Ward, 1939.
HV99.N6.

Loaves and Fishes. San Francisco: Harper & Row, 1983.
 BX4705.D283 A35 1983.
The Long Loneliness: The Autobiography of Dorothy Day. San
 Francisco: Harper & Row, 1952.
 BX4668.D3 A33 1981.
Meditations. Selected and arranged by Stanley Vishnewski. New
 York: Paulist Press, 1970.
 BX2182.2.D36x 1970.
On Pilgrimage: The Sixties. New York: Curtis Books; 1972.

Jessica Powers

The House at Rest. Pewaukee, Wis: Carmelite Monastery, 1984.
 PS3531.09723H68z.
The Lantern Burns. New York: Monastire Press, 1939.
 PS3531.09723L3.
The Place of Splendor. New York: Cosmopolitan Science & Art
 Source Co., 1946.
 PS3531.09723P6.
Selected Poetry of Jessica Powers. Ed. Regina Siegfried and Robert
 F. Morneau. Kansas City: Sheed & Ward, 1989.
 PS3531.09723.

Simone Weil

Cahiers. Paris: Plon, 1951.
 B2430 W473C3 F51.
La Condition ouvrière. Paris: Gallimard, 1951.
 HD6684.W4.
Ecrits de Londres et dernières lettres. Paris: Gallimard, 1957.
 B2430.W471 F57.
First and Last Notebooks. Trans. Richard Rees. New York: Ox-
 ford University Press, 1970.
 B2430.W474 A33 1970.
Formative Writings. 1929–1941. Ed. and trans. Dorothy Tuck
 McFarland and Wilhelmina Van Ness. Amherst, Mass.: Uni-
 versity of Massachusetts Press, 1987.
 B2430.W472 E55   1987.
Gateway to God. Ed. David Raper. New York: Crossroad, 1982.
 B2430.W472E55 1982.

Gravity and Grace. Trans. Arthur Wills. New York: Putnam, 1952.
B2430 W473P43 F52.

Gravity and Grace. Trans. Emma Craufurd. London: Routledge and Kegan Paul, 1963.
B 2430 W473P43 F63.

Intimations of Christianity among the Ancient Greeks. Ed. and trans. Elizabeth Chase Geissbuhler. London: Routledge and Kegan Paul, 1957.
B172.W34   1957.

L'enracinement; prélude à une déclaration des devoirs envers l'être humain. Paris: Gallimard, 1949.
HM216 F49.

Lectures on Philosophy. Trans. Hugh Price. New York: Cambridge University Press, 1978.
B2430.W473 L3513.

Letter to a Priest. Trans. Arthur F. Wills. New York: Putnam, 1954.
194.9 W43L.

The Need for Roots. London: Routledge and Kegan Paul, 1952.
HM216.W352.

The Need for Roots: Prelude to a Declaration of Duties toward Mankind. Trans. Arthur Wills. Boston: Beacon Press, 1955.
HM216.W352   1955.

Notebooks. Trans. Arthur Mills. London: Routledge and Kegan Paul, 1956.
194.9 W43n.

On Science, Necessity, and the Love of God. Ed. and trans. Richard Rees. New York: Oxford University Press, 1968.
B2430.W472E56.

Oppression and Liberty. Trans. Arthur Wills & John Petrie. Amherst, Mass.: University of Massachusetts Press, 1973.
HX266.W3813   1973.

La Pesanteur et la grace. Lausanne: Guilde du Livre, 1948.
BV4833.F48.

Réflexions sur les causes de la liberté et de l'oppression sociale. Paris: Gallimard, 1980.
B2430.W437 R43   1980.

Selected Essays, 1934–1943. Selected and translated by Richard
Rees. New York: Oxford University Press, 1962.
901 W42s.
Seventy Letters. Translated and arranged by Richard Rees. New
York: Oxford University Press, 1965.
B2430.W474A43.
The Simone Weil Reader. Ed. George A. Panichas. New York:
McKay, 1977.
B2430.W472 E55   1977.
*Two Moral Essays: Draft for a Statement of Human Obligations
and Human Personality.* Ed. Ronald Hathaway. Wallingford,
Penn.: Pendle Hill Publications, 1981.
BX7732.P4 240.
Waiting for God. Trans. Emma Craufurd. London: Routledge and
Kegan Paul, 1951.
BV4817.W413.

Ita Ford

Ita Ford: Missionary Martyr. Phyllis Zagano. Mahwah, N.J.:
Paulist Press, 1996.
*Murdered in Central America: The Stories of Eleven U.S. Mis-
sionaries.* D. W. Brett and E. T. Brett. Maryknoll: Orbis Books.
Same Fate as the Poor. Judith M. Noone, M.M. Maryknoll:
Maryknoll Sisters of St. Dominic, 1984. Revised edition.
Maryknoll, N.Y.: Orbis Books, 1995.
Ita Ford's writings were collected and catalogued by Judith Noone,
M.M., for *Same Fate as the Poor;* part of that collection is
located in the Maryknoll Mission Archives.